A SHORT ACCOUNT OF
THE HISTORY OF BURRISHOOLE PARISH

PÁDRAIG Ó MÓRÁIN

a scríobh

ANNÁLA BEAGA
PHARÁISTE BHUIRÉIS UMHAILL

CPR LTD,
Sheeaune, Westport, Mayo, Ireland

This book was originally published by the author in 1957.
This edition is published in Ireland by
Covie Publications and Recordings Ltd, (CPR) 2004.

Copyright © Pádraig Ó'Móráin.

Photograph of Canon Killeen courtesy of Ann Sammon.
All other photographs are from the original copy of this book
and the Moran Family private collection.

ISBN 0-9545740-1-X

Cover design by Hand Eye Studios, Newport, Co Mayo – 098 42135
Printed by Clódóirí Lurgan, Co na Gaillimhe – 091 593251

CONTENTS

Publishers Note	v
Archbishop's Letter	vi
Author and Publisher's Reply	vii
Foreword	ix
1. History of Burrishoole	1
2. Christian Times	7
3. The Parish	9
4. The Abbey	17
5. Some Noted Friars	19
6. Father Anthony Caffrey	25
7. Honoria De Burgo	28
8. Later Christian Times	37
9. Gráinne Ní Mháille	40
10. Tiobóid na Long	42
11. John Browne	44
12. Parson Gouldsmith	45
13. Cromwell	46
14. Catholic Relief Acts	47
15. 18th Century Monuments in Burrishoole	48
16. The Ulster Refugees	50
17. Burrishoole Port	52
18. The Land	57
19. Clann Dálaigh	60
20. The 'Cathach'	66
21. "Who Fears to Speak of '98"	68
22. The 19th Century	77
23. The Famine	81
24. Fenianism	85
25. James Hunter	90
26. Sloinnte: Parochial Surnames	96
27. Log-Ainmneacha: Placenames	99
28. An tAthair Mánus	102

Publisher's Note

Apart from enjoying the company of their lovely son, Seán Nikita, one of the great joys in visiting the home of Pádraig and Maura Doherty in Mulranny, is to talk about books. On one such visit, I was handed an old tattered copy of *A Short Account of the History of Burrishoole Parish.* Pádraig spoke of its author, Pádraig Ó'Móráin, in revered tones. The book was a wonderful read.

With the support of Pádraig Ó'Móráin's two daughters, Dympna Moran from Mulranny and Sheila Sweeney from Achill, it was agreed to re-publish the book through CPR. It could not have happened without them.

This edition includes the letter from Archbishop Joseph Walsh and the reply from Rev Killeen and Pádraig Ó Móráin regarding the 1957 publication.

Thanks are due to both Dympna and Sheila, Máire Sweeney, the Doherty family, Fr Mattie Mc Neely, Evelyn Moran, Mick Moran, Martin Curry, John O'Donahue, Kathleen Duffy, Mary Kelly, Ann Sammon, Mary Alice Reilly, Gerry Bracken, (who was the editor when *The Mayo News* printed this book in 1957), Sr. Consilio, Sr. Immaculata, Pat Treacy and Austin Creaven from Handeye Studios, Tom Hunter and Mícheál Ó'Braonáin from Clódóirí Lurgan, my parents, Joe and Peigí and finally to my anam chara, Gerardine Boyle.

Go raibh maith agaibh go léir.

Liamy Mac Nally,
CPR
Sheeaune, Westport, Co Mayo.

St Jarlath's

Tuam

23rd September, 1957

Rev Thomas Killeen, P.P.
    Newport, Co Mayo

My dear Fr Killeen,

I am very pleased that you are about to publish a history of the parish. To me it seems that the study of local history is a matter of importance for everybody. We are the growth of the past: we have its spirit in our veins; we cannot be good Irishmen if we are indifferent to the language and literature and civilization of our ancestors.

There is a large aspect of this question. Local events may often turn out to be of national interest, and a full history of Ireland cannot be written until every source has been explored.

I congratulate you on the good example you have given by publishing this history.

With best wishes,

✠ JOSEPH WALSH,

Archbishop of Tuam.

Imprimatur:
    ✠ JOSEPHUS,
        Archiepiscopus Tuamensis

Die XXIII mense Sept. anno 1957.

We wish to thank His Grace, Most Rev. Joseph Walsh, D.D., M.A., Archbishop of Tuam for the encouragement he has given, and the interest he has taken in the preparation of this short history of his native parish.

TOMÁS Ó CILLÍN, S.P.
PÁDRAIG Ó MÓRÁIN, M.A.

Foreword

When one endeavours to write the history of a parish community one takes a bold step and submits oneself to the rigours of criticism and the great wisdom of future generations who can look back with the knowledge of the intervening years. When Pádraig Ó Móráin penned Annála Beaga Pharáiste Bhuiréis Umhaill he did so out of love for his native place and a keen interest in that which gave it its particular identity. As a teacher Pádraig Ó Móráin seems to have realised that history is also the school in which mankind learns about itself. As the result of his work, we have today an historical treasure of which the Parish of Burrishoole should feel justifiably proud.

It is with grateful appreciation that the family of Pádraig Ó Móráin acknowledge the help during the research period given by an tAthair Tomás Ó Cillín, S.P., R.I.P. and to the many others, whose names are written in the annals of God. Thank you also to Liamy MacNally whose dedication and persistence has helped to realise the reprinting of the history nearly fifty years after its original publication.

As Pádraig Ó Móráin has shown through his endeavours how the Spirit of the living God has been at work in the history of this West of Ireland parish, we dedicate this reprinting to those who help us today to appreciate the treasure we have within our parish communities.

Sheila Sweeney,
Achill
October 2004

HISTORY OF BURRISHOOLE

"**AT** a point five miles due north of Westport the county road crosses the boundary of the ancient kingdom and the present-day parish of Burrishoole." So writes John O'Donovan. Our guide-book takes on from here and brings us to Newport, two miles further north: "Newport, sometimes called Newport-Pratt, stands at the north-eastern angle of Clew Bay, at the mouth of a small stream called *Abha na Daraí Duibhe* (Black Oak River), which has its source in Lough Beltra.

Both river and lake are well stocked with salmon and trout. Newport Harbour is safe and commodious, and accessible to ocean-going vessels which, the channel being free from bars or sandbanks, can come up to the pier and discharge and take in their cargoes at all states of the tide... North-west of the town, a fine glen extends through the mountains. Bengorm, 1912 feet high, and Buckagh, somewhat higher, tower above it and cast their shadows over Loughs Feeagh (two miles and a half long) and Furnace (a mile and a half long), nestling in the glen; they are so close together as almost to form but one lake. Within easy reach of the town are the ruins of Burrishoole Abbey and of the fortress of Carrigahowley. The abbey ruins retain many tokens of early splendour, some of the mullions and carving being very curious specimens of art. Carrigahowley (Rock of the Fleet) Castle is situated at the extremity of an arm of the sea, with Rockfleet House, on Rossyvera, facing it. Even at low water, a vessel of considerable burthen may ride here in concealment and perfect shelter from the winds. Local tradition tells us that there is an immense hoard of wealth buried beneath the castle, but that it is scrupulously guarded from sunset to sunrise by a mounted horseman who keeps off all marauders ...

Two miles beyond the ruins of Burrishoole Abbey we pass the entrance to the glen of which we spoke already. We have now spread before our eyes one of the most beautiful scenes in the Western Highlands. Clew Bay, with its many islands overlooked on the south by the majestic Croagh Patrick, is to be seen on our left; and the Maum Thomas mountains, of quite a different class of scenery, extend along the right-hand side of the road, their romantic-looking ravines and passes and cliffs inviting a thorough exploration. By the Achill road we reach Mulranny. Mulranny faces Clew Bay, its front windows commanding a view of the inlet and its many islands, chief among them Clare Island in the form of a lion couchant, with Croagh Patrick in the background; and on its west is the strand of Blacksod Bay, which approaches within a few perches of Clew Bay. The village nestles under the shelter of the Maum Thomas mountains, which protect it from the piercing winds of the north and east; this fact, combined with the presence of the Gulf Stream, which laves its front, makes its climate mild and genial, even in the coldest winter."

So ends our guide-book. But more remains to tell. West of Carrigahowley Castle lies Tír an Áir, the land of slaughter, the scene of many a bloody battle in the bad days of old, and now a pleasant land, the home of a kindly people. Further west is Muirbheach, on whose shore is Ross where, when the world was young, dwelt the good-natured fairies of Umhall. Mulranny claims no fairies but it has beauty - the beauty of hill and dale and silver strand. Cushlecka looks on the sea and waits. The *each uisge* (the water horse) will come again of a moonlight night to graze its grassy fields. Two miles further southwest our eyes open in wonder as we gaze on the giant hoof-marks of fabulous pre-historic steeds so clearly outlined on the red rocks of Dumhach Bheag.

From Clew Bay, we turn north to Bealacraher and Binn an Fhiaidh and on by the shore of Blacksod Bay to Dochoill of the changeling. To Dochoill it was that Peadar, the fairy changeling, had come, and there for many a weary month he was nursed and fed. At length he was discovered and died. His funeral to Ballycroy will never be forgotten. The thunder rolled and the lightning flashed and the heavens opened, and the like of that day was never seen before or since. It was as bad as, if not worse than, the burial day of Higgins, the Sham Squire, informer of '98. Dia idir muid agus an anachain.

2

The name of the parish is Buirghéis Umhaill, anglicised Burrishoole, and pronounced locally Bruzoole. Irish-speakers refer it as Paráiste na Buirghéise. Buirghéis comes from the Norman word *burgage,* meaning a town the people of which had certain legal rights and duties.

Shortly after the year 1200, Henry Butler seized the district and built a small town. This was called Buirghéis Cinn Tráchta, that is the burgage at the head of the strand. After some years, the name was changed to Buirghéis Umhaill. The name *Umhall* is very old and remains unexplained. The historical Umhall was the territory now comprised in the parishes of Achill, Burrishoole, Kilmeena, Kilmaclasser, Aghagower, Oughaval, Kilgeever, part of Islandeady, and all the islands from Inishark to Blacksod Bay.

It was divided into two parts, Umhall Íochtair, Lower Umhall, now the barony of Burrishoole, and Umhall Uachtair, now the barony of Murrisk, with the castle of Cathair na Mart standing on the boundary between them. These are the *Two Owels* of the English state papers. Kings of Umhall figure in the Annals. Flannabhra was killed in 773, Flathgal in 786 and his brother, Cosgrach, in 812. Máille, grandson of Cosgrach, is the man from whom the O'Malley family, Clann Máille, are called. Máille had a grand-uncle who was named Fearghus. This is the Fearghus, we believe, who is indicated in the old name of the parish, Leath Fhearghusa, that is, Fergus's half or portion. This was the name of the parish long before the Norman invasion. It is the Latharis of the Papal papers of 1306, 1440, 1463 and of Italian maps of the 14th and 15th centuries. It is not unreasonable to suppose that on the death of his two brothers, Flathgal and Cosgrach, Fergus claimed and got Burrishoole for his share of the kingdom. When the Normans seized Burrishoole in the 13th century there is no mention whatever of the O'Malleys being there. Neither is there any mention of the Fergus family then or at any other time.

The ancient inhabitants of Umhall were Fir Bolg, with likely some pockets of the older race, the Cruithne, here and there. The Fir Bolg were so called from their god, Bolg. The Clann Umhóir tribe of this people settled in Umhall, Galway, and the Aran Isles. Having been conquered by the Goidels

(Milesians), the Fir Bolg were forced to pay tribute. So we find in *Leabhar na gCeart* (Book of Rights, p.99) that every year the King of Umhall had to send to the King of Connacht:

> *"Five score cows of lasting condition,*
> *five score hogs of broad sides,*
> *five score mantles, beautiful their texture."*

There are several interesting references to Umhall in that ancient work, the *Dindshenchus*. The poem, *Carn Conaill,* states that three of Queen Maedhbh's Fir Bolg enemies were buried in the mounds of Magh Find: "hence is named Cnocán na gCeann in strong Ráith Umhaill."

Ráith Umhaill is the pretty hill on which stands the residence of Mr. James Johnson Sweeney. It is now called Roigh. Cnocán na gCeann, the "Hill of the Heads," is close by. The poem, *Druim Criaich,* tells us of nine warriors who fled to Tír Náir, that is to Nár's country. Nár, brother of Queen Meadhbh, was the Fir Bolg King of Burrishoole. The district now named Tír an Áir may have been originally Tír Náir (Nár's country). It is more likely, however, that Tír an Áir, the land of slaughter, is the correct name. Another Fir Bolg chief was Modh. After him our bay is named Cuan Modh (Modh's Bay), and its islands, Inse Modh. How the English "Clew" originated no one appears to know.

Archaeological remains abound in our parish. Circular forts were everywhere. We have already mentioned the famous Ráith Umhaill at Roigh. We can trace at least 24 others. There were forts in Inishkeel, Rockfleet, Ardagh, Carrowbeg North, Beetle Island North, Knockboy (now called Burnt House), Knockglass, Rosgibileen, Milcum, Lecarrow (Lios Míolach), Cuilmore, Lisduff, Derrybrock (Crann na Sídhe), Teevmore. Raith Uí Mhóráin (Moran's Fort), in the grove west of Newport House Hotel, has disappeared. East of Mr. Geoffrey Gibbons's residence at Fauleens are the ruins of a considerable fort. Within the enclosure here are graves of Famine victims. Dr. McEvilly, Archbishop of Tuam, thought it well to come here himself to bless these resting places of the dead. Of the two forts in Roskeen South, one, Lios Mór, has three souterrains, or underground chambers. John O'Donovan writing of Lios Mór, says: "Within it is shewn the site of a small chapel which was probably used during the time of the 'Mountain Masses.'" *(Ord. Survey Letters.* Mayo, 11/4/1838.) In Shanballyhugh there is a fort with two separate underground rooms. The entrance to the rooms is so arranged that the visitor is at the complete mercy of the man inside. Knockglass has one souterrain.

Special mention must be made of Lios na Gaoithe (the Windy Lios), in Letterkeen, at the extreme end of the parish on the border of Tirawley. This, the best preserved ring fort in the district, was excavated some few years ago by Professor Ó Ríordáin and Miss MacDermott of the National University. In it were found graves of the Bronze Age, fully intact and undisturbed, exactly as our pagan forefathers made them 3,500 years ago. Earthenware food vessels were found in each grave, an indication that the people of that time believed in survival after death. The circular fort itself is of much later date. It may have been built in Christian times, even though it is one of the pagan strongholds that figure in the old Mayo tale, Táin Bó Flidais. It was, at any rate, a Christian dwelling place in its later years; the Christian ornaments found there prove that. The builders would seem to have been unaware that they were building over a pagan burial place. The excavation revealed a fine paved entrance to the fort and left no doubt that Lios na Gaoithe was in its heyday a very comfortable home.

The only stone fort we know of in our area was Cahergal (Cathair Gheal). O'Donovan describes it as a "Damnonian fort". The Damnonians were a branch of the Fir Bolg. He says its ruins were there when he visited it in 1838. Nothing of it is to be seen now. In evil times, its stones were used to build houses in Newport.

Some of the curious Standing Stones (Galláin) still remain. They are popularly spoken of as "fir bhréige." What they originally signified is not known. They may have been landmarks. Some of them seem to have marked pagan graves. We have two of these Standing Stones in Rosgalive, two on

Knockalegaun Hill and one on the seashore close by. There is another in Glendahurk and still another in Glenamong.

Every old fort, whether called a *lios,* a *dún* or a *ráith* (the three terms are interchangeable), is generally regarded as a *síodh,* that is, a residence of the fairies. The fairies themselves are the *aos sídhe,* or people of the síodh. There were some forts which they particularly favoured.

One such place is Cnoc Meá near Tuam. In our area, the spot specially linked with them is Ross in Muirbheach, near Mulranny. O'Donovan tells us about them. "At the south-western extremity of Ross-Murvey island there is a hill now sandy but in the memory of Robert U. Walsh it was a beautiful green Shee, called Síodh Muirbhighe. This is the residence of the gentlest and most harmless of the fairies of Umhall, for they were never known to harm men or cattle. Blessings on them.

> *"Sídh Muirbhighe na dtonn*
> *Sídh riamh nach ndearna feall*
> *Sídh aoibhinn na mban fionn."*

> "Shee Murvey of the waves,
> A Shee which was never guilty of treachery,
> A delightful Shee of fair-haired damsels."

CHRISTIAN TIMES

THERE is a hazy tradition that St. Patrick journeyed through our parish. We can be quite certain that he often looked down upon it during his stay on the Reek and blessed it and its people. If Brigid of Kildare was the foundress of the old church of Kilbride, as seems probable enough, we can date the introduction of Christianity to Burrishoole in the beginning of the 6th century.

Marcán of Rossclave was, according to tradition, a contemporary of Brigid. He was certainly a very early saint but as he is not mentioned in any of the old lists, it is impossible to fix his period. We are equally without information about Biorróg's date. There are traces of a very early religious foundation at Burrishoole to the east of the Abbey. In the vicinity is St. Biorróg's bed and a holy well called Tobar na Súl, the well of the eyes. This well is still a favourite place of pilgrimage for people with affections of the eyes. Biorróg is the patroness of the well. There are two places named *Crois,* one near the bed, the other near the bridge on the road to the Abbey. *Crois* indicates a high cross set in a churchyard. Kiltarnet, to the north-east and north of Tobar na Súl, likely contains the name of Sarnat (Sarnad), a holy nun who flourished about 700 A.D. She was of the Uí Fiachrach Aidhne of south Galway. No trace of her church remains. Damhnad (Dympna) is said to have lived for some years at Burrishoole in hiding from her vicious father. She later went to Achill and founded there the church now called Kildownat. Eventually, she was forced to flee to Belgium, where her father caught up with her and killed her.

With St. Brendan of Clonfert, who died in 577 A.D., we are on surer ground. Brendan appears to have devoted himself exclusively to the evangelization of his own race, the Fir Bolg. It is no wonder then that he spent a considerable time in this part of the west. In Roskeen, at the spot called after him Cillín Bhléanainn (Bhréanainn), now Killeen, he built a church, probably also a monastery. All that remains today is a shapeless ruin.

His holy well is still there on the seashore. His memory is held in bene-
diction, and his feast day, the 16th May, is a day of pilgrimage and station.
The station consists of visits to the ruined church and the holy well, with
specified prayers. A living tradition tells of Brendan's aid in a time of
danger. A plague of some kind was devastating the country. The people were
terrified. They cried out to the saint to save them: *Bléanainn míorúilteach
idir sinn agus an phláigh* (Brendan of the miracles between us and the
plague). He heard their cry of anguish and kneeling down in his monastery
at Killeen he prayed for the safety of his people. God granted his request and
the plague did not cross the boundaries of Tír an Áir. Under the year 551 the
Annals of Inisfallen record "a great plague, the Crom (or Crón) Connaill." If
this is the plague the tradition refers to, then Brendan was at work in our
parish in 551 and probably for several years before that.

THE PARISH

ORIGINALLY it is likely that Umhall was a separate diocese with headquarters in the monastery at Aghagower (Ached Fobair) "in which are bishops." *(Tirechan's Collections:* Knox. Dioc. of Tuam, etc., 23). At the Synod of Ráith Breasail, 1110 or 1118 A.D., the whole territory of Umhall was included under the diocese of Cong. Cong is simply the older name for the present archdiocese of Tuam (Arch. Hib. III 8,22). Ráith Breasail marks the time when parishes, as we know them, began to be formed in Ireland.

Up to this period, the spiritual needs of the people were attended to in our area by the monks of Aghagower and the various small communities, such as St. Marcan's at Rossclave. The formation of parishes presented no difficulty. The existing civil boundaries became the parish boundaries. So our Latharis became the parish of Latharis, with its boundaries the same today as they were almost a thousand years ago.

A parish calls for a parochial church. The foundation of Burrishoole Abbey is wrongly attributed by one tradition to the O'Malleys (O Heyne writing in 1704) and by another to the Butlers. The truth may be that the O'Malleys built a parochial church and that the Butlers built another later on. There is a document dated 1334 (Knox: Mayo. 345) which states: "There is another church at Owyl, taxed at 6 marks, whose advowson and presentation belonged to the Earl of Ulster (de Burgo), and will belong to his heirs." This church must be the parish church indicated in the Papal Taxation list of 1306 which gives the taxation of Latharis as 6 marks (Knox; Dioc. of Tuam, etc., 198). The amount of the tax shows that the parish was of considerable importance in those days.

The parish church was no other than the old ruined building we now call Teampall Cúl le Gréin. Pococke writing in 1752 refers to this old teampall "as the ancient Parish Church of Burrishoole, removed, by an act of Vestry and Council, to a glebe about a furlong above Newport on the opposite side." A church that was "ancient" in 1752 was certainly not built

9

by the Protestants. What happened in every place happened here also. The Catholics were evicted and left churchless while their place of worship was turned over to Protestant use.

There are only a few of the names of the early parish priests on record. William de Angulo (Costello or Nangle) was rector in 1413. He was transferred to Castlebar that year. The Pope appointed William de Burgo in his place. John Butler was parish priest in 1440. On his death, the Pope assigned "Burrishoole alias Latharis" to Rauricus O Mearayn (Ruaidhrí Ó Móráin). In 1443, Lewis Ó Hubain became vicar on the death of Cristinus Orilile (O'Reilly). Lewis died in 1454. By command of the Pope, "The vicarage of Burrishoole alias de Latharis" was then given to John de Burgo.

Between 1454, when John de Burgo was appointed to the parish, and 1591 the parish priests are not recorded. Bodkin's "visitation" of 1559 mentions Burges Wyll as one of the livings "usurped by Wyllyam Keighe, although there are others unto whome the same are granted" (Knox. Dioc. of Tuam, etc., 207). The "others" are not named. This Wyllyam is the man known to history as William Burke, the Blind Abbot, brother of Riocard an Iarainn. He was one-eyed or blear-eyed but he was not blind, and he was neither abbot nor priest. We must not regard him as a sacrilegious robber. He and other Catholics of his time seized parochial revenues to prevent their falling into the hands of the Protestants and to insure that the persecuted Catholic clergy had some means of support.

It is likely that William and the others did not lose by the transaction. A list of the clergy of Tuam drawn up probably in 1591 gives Hubert Óg as rector and David Ó Hubain as vicar of Burrishoole. Knox thinks these two were priests but as the list is an entirely Protestant compilation it is more likely they were Protestant ministers (Knox, op. cit. 223-6).

Fr. Teige Hubbane of Carrigeneady is recorded as parish priest in the Registration List of 1704. He was still living in 1715 as his name does not appear in the Grand Jury Presentment of that year (Burke op. cit. 431). His successor seems to have been Fr. Thomas Mulchrone. A vivid local tradition tells of the murder of a Fr. Mulchrone by his nephew and a servant boy in the dim and distant past. The details of the crime have been lately found in the old Dublin newspapers of 1752. Extracts from these papers have been printed in *Archivium Hibernicum,* vol. XVI, 1951. Fr. Mulchrone was murdered in January, 1752. His nephew, Thomas Macanally, and a Marcus Brown were tried for the murder at Castlebar Assizes on 6th September, 1753.

Brown was found guilty and sentenced to be hanged at the spot in Newport where the foul deed had been done (this spot was near the Mill House on the Newport-Castlebar road). Macanally was acquitted "for want of evidence but is ordered for transportation." At the Assizes of 23rd April, 1754, "Thomas Macanally, who was formerly tried for the murder and robbery of his uncle but acquitted for want of evidence and ordered for transportation, was tried for breaking gaol and being at large before the time limited, of which he was found guilty and sentenced to be executed on Saturday, 11th May next." *(Arch. Hib.* vol. XVI 85-86).

We do not know whether Rev. Myles Gibbons was Fr. Mulchrone's immediate successor. We do know that Fr. Gibbons was parish priest of Burrishoole in 1776. A chalice belonging to Aghagower parish bears the inscription: *Me fieri fecit Milerius Gibbons parochus de Borrysoull pro parochia de Aughagower* 1776. *Ora pro eo* (Myles Gibbons P.P. of Burrishoole had me made for the parish of Aghagower 1776. Pray for him). In 1783 Fr. Gibbons, now a Canon and Vicar Forane, compiled a book of prayers and instructions for his people. The M.S. is now in the British Museum. It is mostly in Irish, in a phonetic spelling of the Canon's own invention. The title page reads: "Morning and Evening Prayers together with some instructions before Mass by way of Prone. October 20, 1783. An appendix also wherein the Holy Mass, its parts and the ornaments are explained. There are some instructions and quotations prefixed and interspersed which ought to be carefully read and attended to." The French word *prone* means "preaching, altar notices;" "Ornaments," probably vestments. The instruction on the Mass is superb. He is eloquent on the Rosary. His own profound love for that prayer shows all through while he assumes in his hearers a devoted attachment to it. He adds many beautiful prayers. This seems the only written work by a priest of the Archdiocese of Tuam that has come down to us from the Penal period. In Miss Staunton's house in Newport there is a broken slab with a partly obliterated inscription: *Domus mea Domus Orationis Matt.* 21 13. *M. Gibbons erexit* 177. *Died December* 13, 1792. *Pray for him.* The tablet of erection was used to record his death. We do not know what figure to put after 177. It is clear that the church to whose erection Hugh O'Donnell subscribed £10 in 1752 lasted only some 20 years. The church of 177- stood where Mr. Dominick Kelly now has his residence.

Fr. Peter Waldron was the next parish priest. He, too, set about building a new church. Sir Neal O'Donnell gave a free site on Barrack Hill, where the building was erected in 1803. Patrick Lynch *(Annals of Irish Harps,* 247) says that on 23rd May, 1802, he saw there the shell of a good new chapel. This chapel, with its successor built in 1918, figures in the extraordinary prophecies of Brian Carabine. Brian slept once on Barrack Hill and in the morning said to his son: "In years to come a church will be built on this hill and the altar will stand where I myself slept. But it will come to pass that of that church not a stone will be left upon a stone."

And so it has happened. In 1918, the old church of St. Joseph was demolished to the very foundations. Brian Carabine's period was the last half of the 17th Century. He was a contemporary of the pervert Killala priest, Pól Ó hUigín, who, we know, was a professor in Trinity College, Dublin, in 1685. The builder of this church of prophecy, Fr. Waldron, unlike his curate, Fr. Manus Sweeney, kept strictly aloof from all revolutionary activities. We find him in November, 1798, claiming as a "suffering loyalist" for a mare which some of his patriot parishioners had commandeered for the "Castlebar Races." He left Newport before 1806 and was made Bishop of Killala in 1814.

Rev. John Bourke became parish priest on the departure of Fr. Waldron. Dr. D'Alton (Tuam II, 334) mentions Frs. W. Cusack and Coen as parish priests of Burrishoole with uncertain dates. The truth is that Fr.

Cusack was parish priest of Oughaval 1803-1812 (Memorial slab in Murrisk Abbey). Fr. Coen was Provincial of the Franciscans. He died in Newport, Mayo, 6th September, 1803 (Jennings, I.E.R. July 1951). Fr. Bourke was probably a native of Burrishoole. He was a nephew of Col. Austin O'Malley of '98 fame. He was P.P. till 1830, when he retired from parochial work. But his name, John Canon Bourke, continues to appear in Tuam Chapter lists till 1846. While P.P., it can be said that he devoted himself with zeal and energy to his work.

He built more than eight schools, three in Newport, one each in Lettermoghera, Roskeen, Kiltarnaght, Gortfahy, Carrickaneady, as well as some smaller schools. In 1806, by a levy of 5/5 on each householder, he realised £134 needed for the completion of the new church. In 1813, it was found necessary to ask for a further 10/- per house. When Sir Neal Beg O'Donnell heard of the 10/- per house contribution, he got on his "high horse" and in an open letter to Fr. Bourke, in the *Mayo Constitution* and the *Correspondent,* he charged the priest among other things with misuse of chapel funds. Fr. Bourke immediately called a public meeting and presented his accounts for all and sundry to examine. The examination revealed that every penny of the 5/5 levy of 1806 was fully accounted for and properly expended. In three resolutions the meeting put on record that they were thoroughly satisfied with Fr. Bourke's use of the money, that the 10/- contribution was now absolutely necessary (Sir Neal O'Donnell and Jos. McDonnell to be treasurers), and that they were proud of their "worthy and admirable Pastor." Sir Neal was present and carefully scrutinised all the accounts. He had to admit he had made a grave mistake in accusing Fr. Bourke of misappropriating church funds.

He pledged himself "to correct his error in the same public manner in which the charges were brought forth and to submit the same for my (that is, Fr. Bourke's) approval previous to publication." O'Donnell, however, went back on his pledge and refused to retract. On his refusal, Fr. Bourke sent the whole correspondence to the Dublin *Evening Post,* where it was published on 14th October 1813.

Sir Neal's open letter of 27th Sept., 1813, makes it clear that the baronet's many attempts to "run" both parish and parish priest had not been very successful. Not even from "the lord of the soil" would Fr. Bourke accept any dictation. The decision to ask 10/- per house without consulting him was only the end of a series. The letter is just a mere farrago of pompous abuse. He accuses the priest of scorning his "advice," of forgetting "decency," of denying "essential qualities"(?), of terrorising the people by a system of "black-letter," of fulminating against himself (Sir Neal) in a three-hour oration, false and scandalous, from the altar, of exacting money, a guinea first, then 5/-, then 10/- and now an edict for 10/- more, using funds collected for the chapel for other purposes, giving no account of moneys received, putting a minor out of his property, taking forcible possession of freehold property, substituting a witness's name in a will after the testator's death, refusing to offer £50 on behalf of the parish to find out the persons "that put up notices in Castlebar...My family gave more than £300 to the chapel and I gave my mite. I will place you before a jury of your country."

Fr. Bourke's reply in the Dublin *Evening Post* is very long and very pungent. He says he himself had called for the examination of his accounts before Sir Neal ever thought of it, that since he came to the parish he had made only one collection, the 5/5 of 1806, every penny of which is accounted for, that he has not, as alleged, disgraced the sanctuary by attacks on Sir Neal, that he has given absolutely no cause for Sir Neal's enmity, although the fact that Sir Neal appeared two Sundays "in my chapel to harangue my flock during Divine Service, attempting to lessen me in their esteem" was most provocative, that it is a base falsehood to say that he (Fr. Bourke) substituted the name of a witness on a will after the testator's death, that he has not taken forcible possession of anyone's property nor robbed a minor, that he is executor of Kilcoin's will and will do his duty therein, that Sir Neal can have a copy of that will but not the original, that whatever his accuser may do, he (Fr. Bourke) will act as executor whenever he is asked to do so, that it is evident that the real reason of the anger is his refusal to hand up the Kilcoin will. Fr. Bourke concludes by saying that his consent to the appointment of Sir Neal as one of the joint treasurers of the chapel funds is now withdrawn and that he will not in future tolerate any interference direct or indirect on the part of Sir Neal in Church matters.

What happened after that is not recorded. Fr. Bourke's courage in fighting the "lord of the soil" in those days of ascendency deserves to be recorded. Most probably the two were reconciled later. Sir Neal was a hot-headed blunderer. I think it was about the same time that this great respecter of the law got a year in gaol for some undefined assault. Fr. Bourke seems to have retired in 1829 or 1830. On Monday, 1st March, 1830, Rev. James Hughes was present as Parish Priest at a Vestry meeting in the Protestant church. In those days, before the introduction of the Grand Jury system and the Poor Law, the Protestant Vestries were the authority dealing with public matters such as roads, welfare of the poor, public health, etc. The parish priest had to attend the Vestry meetings on behalf of his flock, who had to supply the necessary funds. We find him at another Vestry (4th June, 1832), at which he was appointed officer of health along with Sir R. O'Donel, Rev. W. Baker Stoney, A. Hoban and Huston Nixon. The Rev. Mr. Stoney was later his opponent at a public religious disputation in Castlebar. This was on the same lines as the famous disputations of the Rev. Mr. Gregg and Fr. Tom Maguire, no quarter given or taken. A verbatim report of the contest was published in book form. In the parish the event was celebrated in a fine Irish ballad and to this day Fr. Hughes remains a mighty figure in local tradition. He often crossed swords with Sir Richard O'Donnell. He is credited by the old people with well-nigh miraculous powers. He was, without doubt, a very able man and an energetic pastor. He was responsible for the opening of several schools in the parish, Newport Boys' School in 1832, Knockmoyle in 1835, Carrowsallagh, Roigh and Mulranny. Lewis (*Topographical Dictionary,* 1837, vol. I, 233) says there were 1,300 children attending the parish schools. In addition, there were 30 children at a hedge school at Carrickaneady. Fr. Hughes was transferred in 1839 to Claremorris, where he died in 1852.

Fr. Hughes was succeeded by Rev. Peter Cannon, who was living in

Clareview Cottage in 1846. On Fr. Cannon's transfer to Kilcommon in 1847 Fr. Matthew Flannelly became P.P. of Burrishoole. In 1856, this priest took in hands the renovation of the church. A new roof was put on and a belfry added. While the work was still unfinished Fr. Flannelly met his death by drowning, 30th June, 1857. His successor was Fr. Richard Prendergast. A kindly, friendly man, Fr. Richard is still fondly remembered in the parish. In his time, the old custom of giving dinner to the clergy at the Stations was abolished, as he felt it involved undue expense on the people's part. Shortly before his death the Sisters of Mercy from Westport opened a branch house and a girls' school in Newport.

On Fr. Richard's death (June 28, 1883), Fr. Patrick Grealy was appointed to the parish. Fr. Grealy was a man who never spared himself. His methods were often drastic but no more so than the situation called for. He is well remembered for his insistence on a full knowledge of the Catechism. Every Station turned out to be for young and old a long session of religious teaching. To the schools he devoted special attention and several new schools were established at his instance. In 1905, the Church of the Immaculate Conception at Mulranny was erected. While yet Bishop of Clonfert, Archbishop Healy of Tuam had on one occasion been refused permission to celebrate Mass in any of the public rooms of the Railway Hotel. He then determined that, if ever he became Archbishop of Tuam, he would have a church built in Mulranny. He did not forget. As soon as he became Archbishop, he instructed Fr. Varden, C.C., to take the work in hands. Canon Grealy died in 1910. Canon MI. McDonald, who succeeded, built the beautiful new church of St. Patrick, which was dedicated 8th September, 1918, by Archbishop Gilmartin. In 1920, two wings were added to St. Brendan's Church, Tiranair. In 1926, the Sisters of Mercy were given charge of Mulranny National School. Shortly afterwards the Mulranny church was enlarged. In 1930, Canon McDonald purchased the old Wesleyan church, where of a day Sir Richard O'Donnell, the Darbyite, used to preach. The building is now converted into a parochial hall. The Canon died 3rd May, 1940.

THE ABBEY

"RICHARD, son of Thomas a Búrc, resigned his lordship." *(Annals of Connacht, 1469).* "Mac William Burke, i.e., Richard, died, having previously resigned his lordship for the sake of God." (A.C., 1473). Richard, called "of Turlough," founded Burrishoole Abbey in 1469 and retired there himself that same year while as yet it was only a wooden house. The Archbishop of Tuam, Donat Ó Murry, had given his permission but as the sanction of the Holy See was necessary, the foundation was irregular. In February, 1486 Pope Innocent VIII regularised the position. In an Apostolic Letter to Archbishop William Joy of Tuam the Pope said he had received a Petition from Donald Ymearan (Ó Móráin), a Dominican, in which it was set forth that Richard de Burgo for the good of his soul had given a plot of ground in Burgos Vaill, named Carta Gracilis (Carrowkeel), for the erection of a convent. His Holiness now gives power to the Archbishop to absolve from excommunication and irregularity all those who began the work without proper sanction. A salutary penance is to be imposed. Full Papal approval is now given to the foundation. It will have all the rights of a properly constituted Dominican convent with a church in honour of, and under the invocation of, the Blessed Virgin Mary and everything necessary for conventual life.

There is little that can be said about the convent buildings. The only part that remains comparatively intact is the church. The convent proper where the friars dwelt has disappeared, the only portion remaining being the ruins of what must have been a beautiful cloister. There is not a trace of the convent cemetery or of any friar's grave. The church originally had no tower. It consisted of the main church which was a plain commodious edifice with high walls and of a Lady chapel on its south side. The tower is evidently of later construction. It fits in badly with the rest of the building and quite spoils the nice stonework of the Lady Chapel. Sidney made a fortress of the abbey, the Cromwellians stormed and captured it, Ormond did his best to put an end to it, but all through it stood intact till, in the year of Marie Antoinette's execution, its roof at length collapsed and left us what John O'Donovan called "a very fine ruin in the Gothic style."

We have no record of the suppression of the Abbey. Malbie placed a garrison of a captain and 100 men there in 1580. The Acta Cap. Gen., 1656, refer to "the heretics who had made the convent a den of thieves," (Mon. Dom. VIII, 475) in Elizabethan times. This is the garrison that captured Father Thady Ó Duane. Probably when these soldiers evacuated the buildings on their conversion to Catholicity no other garrison was sent there. There were no military in the abbey in 1606. The Burrishoole guard mentioned in the State Papers (James, 1608-1610 and 1615-1625) was stationed not in the abbey but at the house where the late Mr. Ernie O'Malley lived. It was in that house Theophilus Bolton, later Protestant Archbishop of Cashel, was born. His father was in command there. Whether the friars had returned to their convent in the time of James I of England we do not know, but the Kelly altar-tomb of 1623 suggests that they had. In 1640 they were in full possession. Cromwell evicted them in 1653. They were back again in 1660 and remained till 1698. If they lived there after 1698 it was not in peace. The fall of the church roof in 1793 means the approaching end of the community.

SOME NOTED FRIARS

IN 1633, Edmund de Burgo, nephew of the reigning Mac William, became a lay brother in the convent. He was a very holy man. His austerities remind us of Matt Talbot. He wore an iron chain as a belt next to his skin and slept on the bare ground or on some straw with a rough stone for a pillow. He allowed himself only a few hours sleep each night. The rest of the night he spent in prayer. In winter, he went barefooted. He used to scourge himself with nettles and sometimes he rolled his body among briars. He had an intense devotion to the Rosary. He was admired for his exemplary life, even by the heretics who had made his convent a den of thieves. He died at a ripe old age (Mon. Dom. VII, 475).

Father Thady Ó Duane of Sligo was the priest who received Honoria de Burgo into the Third Order of St. Dominick. He was long associated with Burrishoole. He lived to see Malbie's garrison in possession of the beloved convent but he set out to do something about it. He was captured by soldiers and brought in as their prisoner. Did he fall into their hands by accident or design? At any rate, he made the most of his captivity by converting every single member of that heretical garrison to Catholicity. This must have been after September, 1592, for Bingham spent two nights there, seemingly with the guard, in that month. The converted soldiers all left the abbey and scattered over the country among the Catholic people (Hib. Dom. 521).

Father Thady Ó Heyne was another who deserves to be ever remembered. He was professed in Burrishoole and was attached to that convent all his life. He lived through the ups and downs of the reigns of James I, Charles I and the tyrant, Cromwell. He never left the country. He was remarkably successful as a catechist. Hunted from post to pillar in the terror and danger of the Cromwellian period, he worked fearlessly among the people and died full of years and fortified by the Holy Sacraments in his beloved convent in 1682 (Coleman; Ó Heyne 220).

Father Walter MacGibbon was another distinguished son of

Burrishoole. He studied in Spain and afterwards he was professor of philosophy, and later of Holy Scripture, in Louvain. Returning home, he became an assiduous preacher. He was prior of Urlar, Straide and last of all, of his native convent of Burrishoole, where he died in 1648.

Father Richard O'Kelly was prior of Burrishoole in 1649. We infer that he was a native of the parish. He took a prominent part in the public life of his time. He is one of the signatories to the petition of the clergy of the Diocese of Tuam against the Treaty with Inchiquin (Rinn. Com. In 62). In the Cromwellian persecution he managed to escape to the continent. He was present, in 1656, at the General Chapter of the Dominican Order in Rome. There with Fr. Felix O'Connor he testified to the martyrdom of the Sisters Honoria de Burgo and Honoria Magaen. After a number of unsuccessful attempts to return to Ireland, he at length, in January, 1660, got on board a Dutch ship bound for Dublin (Arch. Rib. XV 35). He was never heard of again.

Fr. Felix O'Connor was Prior of Burrishoole from 1650 to 1653. When the Cromwellians captured the abbey he made his escape in a dugout canoe to Clare Island. There, a few days later, he fell into the hands of the enemy and was exiled. In the following May, he writes that the Supreme Council condemned him thrice to exile because of his obedience to the Nuncio and that the heretics exempted him from all quarter (Spic. Oss. I 398). In spite of the great danger of the times, he tried often to return to Ireland. He was just one of the heroic priests of whom John Veruiys in a letter dated 28th January, 1660, says: "All indeed show themselves ready to go to Ireland whenever they are assigned thereto by the Sacred Congregation or by their superiors." (Arch. Hib. XV 35-6). Fr. O'Connor did get to Ireland. There, after long years of labour and suffering, he died a prisoner in Sligo gaol in 1679 (Coleman: Appendix 102).

In 1652 there died in Burrishoole Father Thomas Philbin. He was one of those who, while "they fearlessly relieved, by the ministration of the Last Sacraments, Irish Catholics infected by the plague, were themselves struck down and, in a happy agony, gave their lives for their friends." (Acta Gen.

Cap. Rome, 1656). This is the plague of 1652 which struck the Cromwellians in Galway so hard that they proclaimed the 30th December of that year as "a day of fast and prayer and humiliation before the Lord." The plague raged all through the West.

Another Fr. Thomas Philbin became Prior of our convent on the exile of Fr. O'Connor, but he had no convent to live in. He was present at the Chapter of the Dominicans held at Urlar, Co. Mayo, on the 16th August, 1654, in the very height of the Cromwellian terror. His worth in the Order was recognised by the Master-General, who directed that, if Fr. O'Hart, the Provincial, were impeded, the authority would go to Father Philbin. He was still alive in 1696.

At the beginning of the Confederation period, in 1642 probably, the Dominicans opened a school at Burrishoole. The founder of the school was Fr. John O'Hart, Master of Theology. He had to leave his native Sligo on the entrance of the heretic army. In this school he took on the training of the youth, both secular and regular, in the Humanities (Coleman 238). This work of education was of course interrupted in the period 1653 to 1660. In the latter year, it was resumed and, in the midst of untold difficulty, continued till 1697. It was a school which was "of incalculable use to the whole county of Mayo." One doubts whether the school was in the convent buildings. In 1666 the Dominicans and Franciscans were being hunted everywhere by the Government, and in the years that followed many of them were imprisoned, including Fr. John O'Hart (See Burke: *Irish Priests in the Penal Times,* 9-23). The law of 1697 meant the end for our school. That law ordained that all archbishops, bishops, deans, archdeacons or vicar-generals, and all regular priests and members of religious orders were to leave the country. If found in Ireland after a certain date they would be imprisoned or transported (Hayden & Moonan 363).

One of the professors of the Burrishoole school was the celebrated Father John Ó Ruane. He was a fine poet as well as a great scholar. When he was at Burgos in Spain in 1641 the remains of Cardinal Fernando of Austria were being brought home for burial in the Escurial. It was the

21

custom then at such funerals for each religious order to read out publicly before the whole assembly verses in Latin and Spanish praising the virtues of the deceased. Fr. Ó Ruane was selected to write the verses for the Dominican Order, and was excused from choir and matins for the purpose. It was expected that the work would take him the whole night. His Prior was beside himself in the morning when he discovered that Father Ó Ruane had slept the sleep of the just all night and had composed no verses at all. But he assured the Prior that the day was not lost yet. After a few moments of thought, he handed to his superior just two lines of verse:

Austria me genuit, fovit Castella, galerum
Roma dedit, Belgis rector et Hector eram.

That is: Born in Austria, Castile reared me, Rome gave me the (Cardinal's) hat, to the Belgians I was a ruler and a champion.

"When this was read in the presence of the Most Illustrious Lord Archbishop all the company in silence wondered at its excellence." Fr. Ó Ruane got permission to return to Ireland in 1660. From that year we may date the revival of the Burrishoole college. There he taught for his remaining years. He led an exemplary life and died in 1674 amid the blessings of a grieving people.

In 1683, Ormond advised his son, the Earl of Arran, "to have the mad friar at Burrishoole indicted upon the statute in force against such as shall be found in the act of saying Mass and prosecuted to the utmost extent of the law ... The nuns are silly creatures, yet they must be dispersed ... Those priests and friars who governed the ceremony of admitting a new nun ought to be prosecuted. When I mention dispersing the nuns, my meaning extends to the friaries (friars) also." Arran replied a week later, 8th Sept., saying that those at Burrishoole had been fined £50 apiece at the Assizes, which they must pay before they can get out of goal (Burke, I. Priests).

In spite of Ormond and his son, the work continued at Burrishoole. Ormond's "mad friar" we identify with Fr. William de Burgo Junior, who

22

ANNÁLA BEAGA PHARÁISTE BHUIRÉIS UMHAILL

A Short Account of the History of Burrishoole Parish

PÁDRAIG Ó MÓRÁIN

a scríobh

An MAYO NEWS a chlóbhuail ar son na bhfoilsitheoirí

The Original Book Cover.

Pádraig Ó Móráin, M.A.

Rev Thomas Killeen, P.P. This kind and saintly man was a close friend of Pádraig Ó Móráin. They worked together on this book and Canon Killeen published the first edition in 1957.
A great scholar and humble servant of God, Canon Killeen is still remembered with great fondness and deep affection in the parish.

Morning Prayer with Mass for the Dead

on the occasion of the funeral of

Very Rev. Thomas Canon Killeen
Retired Parish Priest of Newport

Friday, December 19th, 1980

Ordained ... ... June 2nd, 1917

C.C., Finney ... ..., ... 1917 - 1921

C.C., Mulranny ... ... 1921 - 1933

C.C., Balla ... ... 1933 - 1935

P.P., Aran ... ... 1935 - 1948

P.P., Newport ... ... 1948 - 1972

Died ... ... December 16th, 1980

Ar dheis De go raibh a anam.

*St. Patrick's Church, Newport, Railway Bridge
and Black Oak River.*

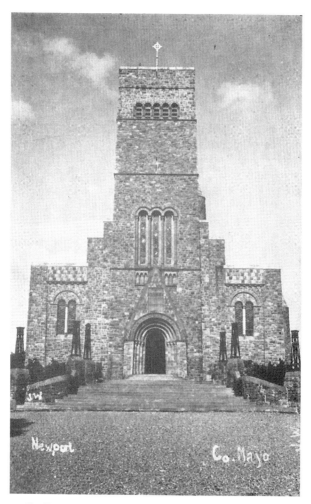

St. Patrick's Church, Newport, erected 1918.

Church of St. Brendan, Tír an Áir, erected in 1810 by John McLoughlin of Newfield House, Tír an Áir, and enlarged in 1920 by the Rev. Canon MacDonald, P.P., Newport.

Oratory of Our Lady, Queen of Martyrs, dedicated to God by his Grace, Most Rev. Joseph Walsh, D.D., M.A., Archbishop of Tuam, on the Feast of Our Lady of Dolours, 15th September, 1954.

was Prior of Burrishoole 1683-1686 and again 1689-1692 and a third time 1695-1698. He was a native of the parish, and of the sixth generation in direct descent from Richard of Turlough, who founded the abbey. He entered the Order at Burrishoole and was professed there. He was a most learned and distinguished man. He was Provincial of his Order in Ireland for two terms in succession-1674-'78 and 1678-'82, being the only friar of his convent to reach that high dignity. Before his return to Ireland he had been a noted figure on the continent. While senior professor of theology at Louvain he had, in a brilliant public thesis, defended the doctrine of the Infallibility of the Pope. For that, he was bitterly attacked by the Jansenists, who stopped at nothing in their efforts to discredit him and his fellow Irish Dominicans. The storm of public abuse and hatred left him quite undisturbed. He was preparing himself for a much more dangerous conflict in his native land. It is strange that it could be said of a man of his parts that when he did come to Ireland his preaching was surprisingly timid. But he soon conquered that and became the foremost preacher in Irish of his day. The dispersal of his community and the abandonment of his beloved convent of Burrishoole following the savage law of 1697 must have broken his heart. A hunted fugitive, he lived on till 1701, when he died in the peace of God.

Another friar who taught in the Burrishoole school was Fr. Walter Gibbons. He lectured there continuously from 1683 to 1696. Another helper was Fr. Walter Johnin (Jennings). Fr. Peter Canavan was assisting in 1696. Fr. Edmund O'Malley was sub-prior from 1683 to 1689. The friars were dispersed in 1698. They were back again in 1702. They had not left the country as the Government had commanded them to do. They had gone into hiding. One of them, Fr. James Collins, was captured and, after a long period in Galway goal, transported to the continent. He returned almost immediately, as we find him again at work in Ireland in 1702. That year, too, Fr. Patrick Walsh was appointed Prior of Burrishoole, and given power to receive novices. How novices could be trained in those days of inhuman persecution is a mystery, but somehow or other, in spite of Government and priest hunters, God's work was carried on. In 1739, the Provincial of the Dominicans was arrested as a spy. Among the papers found on him was a list of the community of St. Mary's, Burrishoole. The list shows eleven of the friars in Ireland and five absent in Europe. The community had 10 silver chalices and nine ornaments (vestments?). Letters were to be addressed: "James Southeast, Newport, for Pat Walsh, Borrisoule." (Fottrell Papers, Louth Arch. Jour., 1930). One of the ten chalices, now in Clifden, is inscribed: *Orate pro anima Petri Browne qui me fieri fecit pro Conventu de Burisowle, A.D. 1724* (Pray for the soul of Peter Browne who got me made for the Convent of Burrishoole). Peter died in 1723, leaving a son, John, then 14 years old. The young heir was, it seems, a Catholic. But in a letter dated 15th April, 1725, the Protestant Archbishop Synge says he has arranged that "the young Mr. Browne be sent to Oxford so that he may be secure from the insinuating attempts of his Popish kindred" (Burke op. cit. 247). It was a clear case of kidnapping. From Oxford, John returned a Protestant. Another of the chalices is in Newport and is inscribed: *Orate pro anima Joannis Brown qui me fieri curavit ad usum Conventus de Burishowle 1723*. This Brown was probably John Brown FitzGeorge of Aughagower. The chalices indicate some kind of community life in Burrishoole in 1723. But in 1731 the Lord's Committee Reports state that of the 20 friars of the convent five were in foreign parts and the remainder dispersed about the country. De Burgo says there were only five friars working in the Burrishoole district in 1756. Fr. Dominic McDonnell was Prior in 1785. He died suddenly on the roadside near Newport on the Mulranny road. On a monument erected on the spot O'Donovan read this inscription: *Rev. Domk. McDonnell sudden death August 1, 1795. Watch you therefore because you know not the day nor the hour.* (Name Books. Burrishoole). This monument is no longer there. Fr. John MacDonnell was the last Prior, 1798, 1799 and 1800. A Friar Horan lived in the district around 1830. The last friar to take the habit for Burrishoole was John Hughes in 1826. He was a native of Galway and it was in Esker his habiting took place.

FATHER ANTHONY CAFFREY

ANTHONY CAFFRY (so he himself spelled the name; others write it "Caffrey") was evidently a native of Burrishoole. He took the habit 25th Sept., 1776 at Esker, Athenry "for the convent of Burrishoole." He was professed in 1777. He studied at the Sorbonne in Paris. We hear of him again in 1794 in Washington D.C. "Irish labourers ... prevailed on a zealous priest, Rev. Anthony Caffrey, to come from Ireland to assuage their spiritual needs. Fr. Caffrey (or McCaffrey) purchased some lots still in possession of St. Patrick's parish ... He came in 1794, and in 1804 the land purchased was deeded to Bishop Carroll, and Washington knew him no more." (Downing: *Catholic Founders of National Capital*). A letter of his in the Baltimore Archives is dated "Washington, 1 Oct., 1794." In April of that year he had bought the first portion of the property for £140. The people were so poor that it was only in 1798 he cleared the debt; even then he had to use his own personal money. Hundreds of Irish workers who had flocked to Washington for the great building programme projected for the national capital were stranded and impoverished because the work was held up by Congress. Fr. Caffry came to the rescue. He was helped in his work of charity by Catholics, such as his great friend James Hoban, designer of the White House and later architect of the Capitol, and by non-Catholics such as "the fabulous figures, James Greenleaf and Robert Morris, the most ambitious of all the land speculators of the new city." (Clarke: Greenleaf & Law. Wash. D.C.). Having got his site at the corner of 10th and E. Street, he erected there about 1796 the first St. Patrick's (Hines: *Early Recollections of Washington*).

This was a frame building. Before he left the city it seems certain that he had the frame church replaced by the solid edifice that is the present St. Patrick's. "Rev. Anthony Caffrey by a deed recorded on the 10th Sept., 1804, has transmitted to R.R. Dr. Carroll the lot on which St. Patrick's Church stands." (Baltimore Archives). In the same Archives there is a letter written by Dr. Neale, Coadjutor Bishop, dated 27th January, 1804, which refers to St. Patrick's Church. In the light of this, it is impossible to hold, as some students do, that the builder of the church was not Fr. Caffrey but his successor, Rev. William Matthews. The latter only succeeded Fr. Caffrey on the 31st July, 1804.

In the Baltimore Archives there are several letters written by Fr. Caffrey himself and several by others about him. Dr. Neale, the Coadjutor, complains: "Fr. Caffrey insists on the whole city belonging to St. Patrick's." (27th Jan., 1804). Dr. Carroll had decided that the "precincts" of the city belonged to St. Patrick's. Dr. Neale wants the term "precincts" defined, as Fr. Caffrey has interpreted it in his own way as meaning the whole city. We do not know what Dr. Carroll decided. A few months later, Father Caffrey's continuing bad health forced him to resign his charge. He left Washington in the autumn of 1804. He acted as assistant in St. Peter's church in New York for a short period in 1805 (Corrigan: *Historical Records,* 1.207). He was in Ireland when we hear of him again. In 1808, the Irish Provincial Chapter postulated that the Preacher Generalship of Athenry be conferred on "Fr. Anth. Caffrey, aged 45, profession 30, Lie. Sorbonne, who has laboured zealously in America." From Dublin, on the 26th February, 1811, he wrote to Dr. Carroll, now Archbishop of Baltimore. This letter tells of his meeting in Dublin the Archbishop's nephew "who feasted me with a long narration and detailed account of my friends and connections in America." He goes on to say: "I have retrieved my constitution in my native air." He refers to Maynooth in no complimentary way. He mentions the wonderful funeral (convoy he calls it) of the holy Fr. Beaty. He concludes: "I still in the pride of my heart speak of you as my bishop." The letter is signed: "Anth. Caffry. Directions are: Newport-Pratt, Co. Mayo, Ireland."

Back in Newport, we find his name as a land-holder in Derryloughan in O'Donnell's Rent Roll (1810). But it was not for long. He was dead by November, 1811. On the 2nd of that month Dr. Troy, Archbishop of Dublin, sent news of his death to Dr. Carroll. The Archbishop of Baltimore replied to Dr. Troy on 16th Jan., 1812: "Not only my nephew but I likewise feel at a loss to express our acknowledgment to your Grace for the speedy information of the lamented death of his and my good-hearted friend, Dr. Caffrey. R.I.P." (Spic. Oss. 111 533). The obit list of the Ordo of 1813 mentions the death: "Antonie Caffry, S.T.L. Bouroz." Bouroz is a misreading for Burrishoole. So died an able and zealous son of St. Dominic. His grave is unknown. No monument has been raised to his memory either in Burrishoole or in Washington where in labour and pain, he founded the city's first Catholic church. May he rest in peace.

HONORIA DE BURGO

IN the quiet atmosphere of the cloisters, Honoria de Burgo lived her long life from the age of 14 years to her death at 104 years. Perhaps the serenity of her existence was untouched by the tremendous happenings around. On the other hand, it is conceivable that this beginning of religious persecution and intolerance caused many anxious moments to the nuns here, as well as to other religious, and certainly history and contemporary annals refer frequently enough to the burning and desecration of religious houses.

In the Irish Ecclesiastical Record of April, 1918, there is published a "list of those who, it is confidently claimed, died for the Faith in Ireland and whose Cause for Beatification and Canonisation is at present under investigation by his Grace the Archbishop of Dublin, acting by delegation from the Holy See... It should be our earnest prayer that the Holy See, in defence of whose divinely constituted supremacy over all the Church on earth they are piously believed to have died, will find them entitled to the honours of our Altars." The names given number 258. Only those for whose martyrdom there is historical evidence are mentioned in the list. There must, of course, have been thousands of others, both priests and laity, who died for the Faith in those terrible years but whose stories are known to God alone.

Among the 258 there are enumerated six women, namely, No. 99, Eleanor Birmingham who died at Dublin in prison in 1584; No. 156, 157, Elizabeth Kearney and Margaret of Cashel, killed in Cashel in 1647; No. 241, Bridget Darcy, wife of Florence Fitzpatrick of Ossory, hanged in 1652; No. 242, 243, Honoria de Burgo (Burke) and Honoria Magaen, died from hardships at Saints Island, Clew Bay, 1653. The records of the case of Honoria de Burgo and Honoria Magaen are to be found in De Burgo's *Hibernia Dominicana* p. 572 and *Mon. Dominicana* VII p.478. De Burgo is quoting from the Acts of the General Chapter of the Dominicans held at Rome in the year 1656, just three years after the death of the two nuns. The facts were supplied to the Chapter by one of the priests of Burrishoole

Abbey who knew the two personally and who was in the vicinity when the Abbey was attacked and captured from the Confederation forces by the Cromwellians in February, 1653. The maid servant who figures in the story is without doubt the source of all that is known of the last hours of these two holy virgins. The following is a free translation of the Latin of the Acts:

"Year 1653. Sister Honoria de Burgo added to the glowing white of her virginity the purple hue of martyrdom, that thus she might make herself worthy of her glorious but bloodstained Spouse. She belonged to the illustrious de Burgo family of Mayo, her father being Richard de Burgo. At the age of fourteen she was clothed in the habit of the Third Order of St. Dominick, sometimes called the Order of St. Catherine of Siena, by Father Thady O'Duane, O.P., Provincial of the Irish Dominicans. She had a house erected for her near the church of Burrishoole Abbey. Here during the reigns of Elizabeth, James 1 and Charles 1, she lived a life of extraordinary holiness, exercising herself assiduously in the practice of virtue and piety, even in her feeble old age. Those who knew her tell of her marvellous purity and innocence. It is recorded that in one of the frequent famines of the time she and her companion nun were in danger of death from hunger. But God in His goodness answered the fervent prayers of His humble servants. A young man whom they did not know suddenly appeared at their door, bringing with him plentiful provisions. He departed as suddenly as he had come. Who he was, or where he came from, or where he went, no one could tell. They could only surmise that he was an angel of God, sent to help them in their distress.

"With the coming of the Cromwellians monks and nuns were everywhere dispersed and forced to fly for their lives. Honoria de Burgo with her companion and a maid servant fled for safety to a little island in Loch Furnace called Saints' Island. But soon their hiding place was discovered by the enemy. Although it was bitter winter weather (it was February), the savage English soldiers stripped the two nuns almost naked. Honoria de Burgo who was an exceedingly old woman, just skin and bone, was almost frozen to death by the piercing cold. But there was no pity for her. She was dragged to the shore and flung like a bundle of sticks into the boat. The fall bruised and bashed her poor frail body. Three of her ribs were broken. She could not long survive this brutal treatment. But before she died she requested the maid, who seems to have been unmolested by the soldiers, to carry her to the Abbey Church and lay her down before the altar of Our Blessed Lady, that she might die there. The maid took her from the boat and carried her on her back to the Church.

"There she laid the old nun reverently down before the altar. Having done all she could in the circumstances, she went out to search for the other nun who had escaped into the wood. Her search was in vain. She returned to the church. There, to her astonishment, she found Sister Honoria de Burgo, whom she had left lying down before the altar, now kneeling with head erect in an attitude of prayer. But Honoria was dead. No trace remained of the terrible agony she had undergone. Instead, on her face was a look of peace, the unutterable peace of those who die in the Lord.

"Sister Honoria Magaen was also a professed nun of the Third Order. She had been the inseparable companion of Honoria de Burgo and shared in all her labours and sorrows. And now, even in death and in the grave, she could not be separated from her. As we have seen, she, too, was captured in Saints' Island by the Cromwellians. Those ministers of Satan, in their diabolical hatred of the Catholic religion which her habit symbolised, stripped her naked and beat her unmercifully and threw her into the boat. In spite of her many wounds, however, when the boat reached land she managed to elude her captors and escaped into a wood. She was a comparatively young woman and she feared more for her chastity than for her life. She hid herself in the hollow trunk of a tree. There next day she was found frozen to death. She was buried in the same grave with Honoria de Burgo."

The above tells us all we know of the two nuns. There was a much longer account in Rome or Paris shortly after the General Chapter but it has disappeared. It must have been a wonderful story. It so impressed the artist who shortly after, the year 1651 was painting the frescoes of the great saints of the Dominican Order in the cloister of the Dominican Convent in Taormina in Sicily that he deemed the Burrishoole woman (Honoria Magaen) worthy of having her portrait placed in the august company of St. Dominick, St. Thomas of Aquin and the other great saints of the Order. It is our earnest hope, and it should be our earnest prayer, that one day the Church will raise Honoria de Burgo and Honoria Magaen to the honours of our Altars.

Who was Richard de Burgo, father of Honoria? There were several Richards in that period. But it seems likely that Richard an Iarainn de Burgo is the man meant. He married Gráinne Ní Mháille not earlier than 1570. She was the widow of Domhnaill a' Chogaidh Ó Flaherty. Richard was at the time of his marriage to Gráinne rather elderly. The *Four Masters* tells us he was defeated in battle as early as 1553. We are not told that Richard was a widower when he married Gráinne, but from the circumstances of the period we can be practically certain that he was. Honoria then would be a child of his first marriage. Local tradition suggests that so it was: "When the Burkes were living in the castle near Murrays (the track of it is there yet on the top of the hill), the girls of the family used to see a bush where the abbey is now, all covered with white birds every morning for a certain length of time and they said it must be a very holy place. The eldest of the girls asked to get her share. She got it and it was enough to build the abbey. The mortar was poured on hot and that is why the building stood so well. That was the beginning of the nuns at the abbey."

In fact, the abbey was founded in 1469 when as yet there was no castle on the hill. We do not know when the castle was built but at any rate it was here Richard an Iarainn lived all his life. The tradition we have quoted in mentioning a castle confuses the founding of the Abbey with the building of a special house for Honoria de Burgo 100 years later. The account of her life which we have given above says she had a house erected for herself near the abbey, outside, of course, the abbey boundary. If it was in Burrishoole Castle Honoria lived there can be no doubt that Richard an Iarainn was her father.

Father Thaddeus Duane was Provincial of the Dominicans in the years

1560 and 1563. Bishop de Burgo (Hib. Dom. 520) says that Honoria de Burgo who lived to be 104 years old was, in her fourteenth year, clothed with the habit of the Third Order of St. Dominick by the Provincial, Thaddeus Ó Duane, in the year 1563. Honoria then was born in 1549.

Of the other Sister, Honoria Magaen, we know nothing. Local traditions agree in stating that Honoria de Burgo was a native of the parish. The name Honoria is not in any tradition. All that is mentioned is: "A nun named Burke with another nun." The name Magaen may be Mac Aodhain, Mag Aodhain (Nig Aodhain). Locally, MacAodhain gives us Keane, Kane, e.g., Pádraig MhacAodhain which is shortened to Pádraig 'acAodhain. This Sister's name is, however, preserved forever in the fresco of the former Dominican convent in Taormina, Sicily. This convent was secularised by a Freemason Italian Government sometime after 1870 and is now a hotel. It has been confirmed that the cloisters in which this fresco and others were painted, still stands. The pictures are there to this day. The fresco of Honoria Magaen was accidentally discovered in 1921 by Right Rev. Mgr. Curran, now P.P., Aughrim St., Dublin. There is no certain date for the work, but it is agreed that the artist (who is unknown) painted the pictures shortly after the year 1656. It was in that year the General Chapter of the Dominican Order was held in Rome. The actual wording on the fresco is: B. Honoria Magaen D'Ibernia.

The date of the death of the two Sisters is given by the General Chapter as February, 1653. It was in that same month and year Burrishoole Abbey was attacked and captured by the Cromwellians. Fr. Felix O'Connor, O.P., who was Prior of Burrishoole in that year, tells us something about this attack. He had been Prior of Kilkenny but when that city surrendered to Cromwell on 27th March, 1650, he was excluded from pardon. He escaped, however and made his way to Burrishoole, where he was elected Prior. Writing from Brussels on 17th May, 1653, he says:

"After the disaster of Kilkenny I was elected Prior of Burrishoole Convent in the west of Connacht in the area near to the island of Boffin. Here for three years I was constantly giving shelter to other refugee religious. But at length the heretics arrived on the scene. There was not a spot that escaped their attention in the whole country. They attacked our convent but were twice repulsed. A furious third assault succeeded and they burst into the building. They killed all the soldiers I had with me. Of the religious some were made prisoners, some were wounded, while others fled in headlong flight to the mountains. I myself, with one boy, managed to get a dugout canoe and in that tiny boat I launched into the deep. I preferred a thousand times to trust myself to the mercy of the waves rather than to the raging madness of the bloodthirsty Cromwellians. By the grace of God, when everyone thought I would be certainly drowned in that little canoe made of one single tree trunk, I made Clare Island in safety. It was a journey of six leagues on the high seas. In the island I found a few soldiers as well as some of the nobility and ecclesiastics who for many months in their love for the Faith had endured the rigours and hardships of mountains and woods and the attacks of the enemy till they at length were compelled to fly to this island for protection. Here they waited, hoping for God's help in their distress. But it was not long till we saw ourselves surrounded by seven ships of the Parliamentarians with 22 small boats. We were helpless. Without was conflict, within we were hopeless and weighed down with terror. It grieved us to the heart to learn that in desperation, and despair of any help from outside, the tremendous fortress of Boffin, not far from Clare, had been surrendered to the enemy. We in Clare had no option but to yield. They put us in their boats and our sentence was made known to us. It was exile beyond the seas and instant death if we ever returned."

Boffin surrendered 15th February, 1653. One of the conditions was that Clare Island as well be handed over to the English and this was to be done within six days. We infer that Fr. Felix reached Clare Island some days before the 20th February, 1653. The attack on Burrishoole most likely took place about the 15th February. We need have no doubt that the fanatic Roundheads lost no time in hunting out the two women who had escaped before the attack on the Abbey. They had not far to go. Saints' Island is about a mile from the Abbey. It is quite likely that the nuns were done to death on the 15th or 16th of February.

In the short account of Honoria de Burgo it is stated that the other events of her life are to be recorded in a much longer history. This longer history was published and was quoted by Lynch in his *De Praesulibus Hiberniae* II p. 67. Lynch refers to it when treating of Bishop Terence Albert O'Brien of Emly, another martyr of the Cromwellian period. The title of the book was *Rosetum Praedicatorium Hibernicum.* It is said that it has disappeared. It was written by Fr. Denis O'Hanrahan, O.P. All we know about the happenings at Burrishoole and about the two Sisters came without doubt from two Dominican priests, Fr. Felix O'Connor and Fr. Richard O'Kelly. The latter was prior of Burrishoole in 1648. The former, as we know, was prior there from 1650 to 1653. Both, of course, knew the two women well. The Master General of the Dominicans, John Baptist de Marinis, writing in 1655, refers to the two priests as presenting him with an account of the terrible things that had happened in Ireland, of which they themselves were eyewitnesses. He further states that they will publish a full history of what they knew of the tragedy of Ireland.

In the story of the two Honorias we are told that, it was in Saints' Island (insula sanctorum) they were captured. This is a little island in Furnace Lough. Apparently, it was called Island of the Saints long before 1653. We have, however, no tradition of any saint who was connected with it. Such traditions as we have are largely fanciful. The general account says that there was no island there but that when the nuns saw their enemies coming they prayed for protection. Their prayer was answered. The spot on which they stood was suddenly surrounded with water. The people of Shanballyhugh and Cloonfoher, the nearest townlands on the shore of the lake, often saw of a fine day the shadow of the road leading to the spot. Other versions say the island was always there but that when the nuns came to the shore the water disappeared so that they could walk in. When they had got in the water returned and surrounded the island again. All the accounts are at one in saying that two nuns fled from Burrishoole and were pursued by soldiers.

Apart from being English soldiers, nothing else was known. Cromwellians are not mentioned. The following tradition, which we think genuine, is quite circumstantial: "The soldiers got a boat to go in for the nuns. They gave them cruel treatment. One of them was thrown into the boat and her ribs were broken and she got other injuries besides and she died of them. The other nun died, too, from the bad treatment she got. Neither of them died in the island and neither is buried there. One of them was Burke and she was a native of this parish. There was a blessed well in the island one time and you can see the hollow where it was at the foot of the bush. We heard old people tell that the island was a place of pilgrimage long ago, but there went no one to do a station in it during our time (i.e. since 1834). Some of the old people used to hear it called Oileán na Naomh and Saints' Island. The more common name lately is White Island."

The painting referred to previously is oval and about five feet high. The general colour is pale yellow. There are with it six other frescos representing Dominican Sisters. They are Venerable Sister Francesa Alessandra of Sicily; B. Lucia of Narni; B. Caterina of Racconigi; B. Margarita, Duchess of Savoy; B. Hosanna of Cattaro, and Giovanna, Queen of Portugal. Seán Ó Faoláin was in Taormina in 1950. He says: "The cloister (below around the central court or garden) is intact. Around the walls are paintings, i.e., framed pictures." On the other hand, a letter written by the manager on 'Grand Hotel and San Domenico' paper on 14th November, 1951, says: "I have searched, and there is indeed, in the grand corridor on the ground floor of the San Domenico, a fresco on the side, over the door - oval-shaped - and to be exact over the door of the room numbered 104, bearing the following inscription: 'B. Honorata Magean d'Ibernia.' The name of the artist is unknown. The fresco is original and dates from 1640." The manager transcribed the name wrongly. Honoria, not Honorata, is the name on the fresco. He is wrong, too, in the year. It could not be 1640. It is certainly not older than 1656. All the frescos are by an unknown artist. It is impossible to find out who he was as there has never been a descriptive list.

After the capture of Aran in January, 1653, the Cromwellians sent large forces to attack Boffin. "About the 6th February, near Renvyle, 800 Irish fell upon 270 foote which were marching to reduce Boffin." (Gilbert: *History of Affairs in Ireland* VI. p. 370). This action appears to be that mentioned in a letter written by Dr. John Dowley, Vicar General of Tuam, on the 9th March, 1653. The address Dr. Dowley gives is typical of the times: *In loco nostri refugii juxta Cruagh Patrik Dioec. Tuam.* In our hiding place near Croagh Patrick. "After the capture of Aran the English invaded Connemara. They were attacked by Colonel Dudley Costello. In the ensuing fight 100 of the English were killed while the losses on the Irish side were one captain and three or four soldiers killed. But that did not stop the English and they proceeded to invest Boffin." (Sp. Os. I, 305) Dudley continued the fight later on but was captured and executed. The surrender of Boffin appears to have been engineered by Cusack, the commander, who was acting secretly as the agent of the notorious Earl of Ormond. We can understand the consternation of the Clare Island refugees when they saw themselves surrounded by the Cromwellian fleet. Their last hope was centred in Boffin holding out. There is no doubt that it could have for many months defied all the power of the enemy sufficiently long to have given the Confederation army a breathing space to rally their scattered forces and continue the fight with better chance of success. But Cusack surrendered without firing a shot. As has been hinted above, he was afterwards accused of treachery. But he and others were too late in realising that in serving Ormond they were destroying their religion and their country. In after years we find many of those soldiers coming together with the great-souled Murtagh (Muircheartach) O'Brien, who never yielded to the English enemy, to devise plans to get possession again of Aran and Boffin as the best bases for war on Cromwell and his gang. But it was late.

LATER CHRISTIAN TIMES

VERY little is recorded about Umhall in pre-Norman times. In 812 A.D. the Danes descended on the district but were repulsed with slaughter. The next year they returned in force and this time it was the men of Umhall who were slaughtered. Among the dead were Dunadhach, King of Umhall, and Cosgrach, son of Flannabhra. There is a hazy tradition that the whole royal family was wiped out on this occasion and that it was only through a very extraordinary miracle of St. Brendan that the line was preserved. What appears to have happened was that after their victory the Danes dug themselves in and the local chiefs were forced to withdraw from Burrishoole across the bay of Lower Umhall. The Danish stronghold was Iniscoitil. Caitil is the Irish for some Danish chieftain's name. When the Normans invaded Burrishoole they seem to have met with no local resistance. The O'Malleys figure little in the accounts of the period. In later years they are mentioned, but chiefly in records of matrimonial alliances between themselves and the English invaders. Edmund Albanach de Burgo, who died in 1375, had as his first wife Sadhbh, daughter of Diarmaid Ó Máille (I.T.S. XXVII 164). By Papal dispensation Raymund de Burgo married Joan Ní Mháille in 1432. Thady Ó Máille married Sabina de Burgo in 1440. The De Burgo-Ó Máille chalice made in 1494 witnesses the marriage of Thomas de Burgo and Gránia Ní Máille. Last of all Gráinne Ní Mháille, queen of the West, became the wife of Riocard an Iarainn de Burgo in Elizabethan times.

The Normans first landed in Ireland in 1169. Sixteen years later they reached Burrishoole. A Butler chronicler of the 18th century records a tradition that Theobald, son of Walter Butler, who came over with Prince John in 1185 "neither stopped nor stayed till he reached Inishowle in Lower Connacht." On arrival in our district, the Butlers, as was the Norman way, at once built their castle. The site they selected for this building was the hill of Ceann Tráchta, overlooking Clew Bay. Here, too, they founded their town of Burrishoole. The castle, called the Castle of Tyren More in the Annals of

Clonmacnois, was burned by the O'Connors in 1248. In 1272, the O'Connors returned to the attack and defeated and slew Henry Butler, Lord of Umhall, and Hoitse Mebhric, his chief lieutenant. Glenhest is named after this Hoitse. He had, it seems, seized it and made it his own. After this battle the Butlers disappeared from the local scene but the family still held on to the title Henry had claimed for himself, none other than "Lord of Akyll and Owyll in Connacht" (Deeds of 1380 and 1381).

The expulsion of the Butlers gave that other Norman family, the de Burgos, the chance they were waiting for. They immediately descended on Umhall and seized the vacated territory. William Liath de Burgo, who died in 1324, is called "Hero of Umhall" by Tadhg Dall Ó hUiginn. William's grandson, who died in 1343, is called "Ulick of Umhall." A document of 1333 mentions John and William de Burgo as holders of property in the district. As ruler of Burrishoole, Richard de Burgo of Turlough was able in 1469 to grant the townland of Carrowkeel to the Dominicans. To emphasise their over lordship there were in the parish four de Burgo castles. On the hill north of the abbey stood their chief residence, the Castle of Burrishoole, originally built by the Butlers and called by them the Castle of Tyren More. It was here Riocard an Iarainn, the MacWilliam of his day, lived. It was here, too, we think, that Sister Honoria de Burgo was born. On Barrack Hill was Ballyviaghan Castle. In Carrickaneady was another castle, the residence in the 16th century of the MacDonnells, who had come from the Scottish Isles as gallowglasses to the de Burgos. Last of all is Carraig an Chabhlaigh castle, still standing and famous as the fortress of Grace O'Malley.

The de Burgos were all-powerful in the 14th, 15th and first half of the 16th century. Their great defect was their propensity to fighting among themselves. What the Four Masters said about Riocard an Iarainn, who died in 1583, would apply with equal truth to almost every one of them: "a plundering, warlike, unquiet and rebellious man." Their continual internecine feuds so weakened them eventually that the ruthless Bingham found it easy to destroy them. From 1550 on the English pressure began to be felt. In 1566, we see Riocard de Burgo, the MacWilliam, chief of his nation, shamefully kneeling at Sidney's feet, making "his humble submission to the queen." The next MacWilliam, Shane Mac Oliverus, "did his humble homage" to her English majesty in 1576. Sidney tells us that this man spoke only Irish and Latin and was totally ignorant of English. The next in line, Riocard an Iarainn, Mac William 1580-1583, crawled in from the islands and went on his knees in abject submission. His successor, Ricard Mac Oliverus, likewise yielded. He also consented to the abolition of the Brehon law and accepted English law. Bingham would tolerate no more MacWilliams. The de Burgos, or Burkes as they were now being called, broke out in rebellion, as Bingham apparently expected they would. But their cause was hopeless and in the ensuing fighting they were nearly exterminated. The family revived somewhat in the first half of the 17th century. Then came Cromwell and their day was done forever.

GRÁINNE NÍ MHÁILLE

GRÁINNE, daughter of Owen O'Malley, was married twice. Her first husband was Domhnall a' Chogaidh Ó Flaherty of Conamara. Of this marriage there were two sons, Owen Ó Flaherty, who was put to death by Bingham, and Murchadh na Maor, who died in 1626. On the death of Domhnall, Gráinne married Riocard an Iarainn de Burgo of Burrishoole. It is probable that this was Riocard's second marriage also. While her husband lived in Burrishoole Castle, Gráinne chose Carraig an Chabhlaigh Castle as her base of operations. As a wife, she was faithful and no aspersions were ever cast on her character. But her heart was in the fight against the English oppressor. With Carraig an Chabhlaigh as her centre, she set out with her fleet of galleys to harass English shipping, especially in Galway Bay. Her raids proved so troublesome that it was determined to capture her. Captain Martin was sent with a strong force of troops in 1579 to take her castle. Martin got more than he bargained for. His party were repulsed with great slaughter and he himself escaped only with difficulty. Several local placenames derive from this encounter: Crugán an Áir (Crugan of the slaughter), Páirc Dhearg (Field red with blood), Lag na Mallacht (Lag of the curses). Malbie came to Burrishoole the next year, 1580. He does not mention Gráinne, but it was, perhaps, because of her he left a strong garrison in the abbey. In 1586, she was again in arms against the English. She was captured in Galway but was released by Bingham under a guarantee of her son-in-law, Richard Burke, son of the "Devil's Hook" (Deamhan an Chorráin). In 1587, Perrot reported that some of the Mac Swynes sent aid to Granye ne Male (Hayes-McCoy: Scottish Mercenary Forces 66). She raided Aran Isles in 1590. In 1593 she went to England to seek from Elizabeth the release of her son, Tiobóid na Long, and her brother, Domhnall na Pipee, who were in gaol. Elizabeth agreed to set them free, and wrote that "out of pity for this aged woman she desires Sir Richard Bingham to deal with her sons to yield her some maintenance for the rest of her old years." (Knox:

Mayo 254). The "aged woman" had some life in her still. The Dean of Limerick, writing in 1596, says: "MacNeil of Barra and Grany ny Mallye invaded one another's possessions though far distant" (Hayes-McCoy; Ibid. 142). That is the last we hear of Gráinne. Tradition says she died and was buried in Clare Island.

TIOBÓID NA LONG

TIOBÓID NA LONG (of the ships), son of Riocard an Iarainn de Burgo and Gráinne Ní Mháille, was born in Burrishoole Castle about 1570. In 1593, he first became prominent when he was arrested on suspicion of conspiring with Brian O'Rourke. When released by Elizabeth at his mother's request, he set out to prove his loyalty by a murderous campaign against his own relations. In April, 1595, he sent in a list of 16 Burkes whom he claimed he had himself slain (Knox. op. cit. 255). In 1620, he and his son, Miles, were charged with the murder of one Lucopp. At the trial, Miles testified that in Lent a Scottish ship laden with wines, of which Robert Lucopp was owner, came into the bay of Burrishoole. He, Miles, with his wife and others and the servants, were invited on board. His father, Tiobóid, was not on board but met Lucopp in an island near the ship, where they talked about the murder of Lucopp's brother in that place 16 years before. Lucopp and his company came to his house often for dinner and supper. David Bourke, his cousin german with Owen O'Flaherty, Rory McCormack, Tibbot Duffy, Alexander Óg, and Myler Óg did surprise the ship and murder the mariners. Richard M'Gilleduff and Murtagh Roe, one of his servants, fled from the ship when they saw the murder committed. Miles and his father were acquitted. The State Paper (1615-1625) says: "David. . . the principal actor in the murder, and the rest of his confederates, perished miserably at sea."

In 1625, Tiobóid, now Sir Tibbot Burke, and Miles were again in gaol, charged with plotting with the King of Spain (C.S.P.I. Charles I. 1625). They were acquitted. Soon after this, Sir Tibbot was created Viscount Burke of Mayo. A few years later he was dead. He is buried in Ballintubber Abbey.

Miles, second Viscount Mayo, and his son, Theobald, the third Viscount, were both natives of Burrishoole. D'Alton states that Miles apostatised (Tuam I, 256), but produces no evidence to prove his contention. About Theobald, D'Alton says that he did nothing to save the people who were killed in the "Massacre of Shrule" in 1642, and that it was because of this neglect he was ten years later put to death by the Cromwellians. This judgment on a man who was certainly an exemplary Catholic needs revision. It was not because of Shrule that Theobald was shot to death in Galway. He died for his Faith and his name has been found worthy to be included in the list of those whom the Irish Church has requested the Holy See to honour as martyrs.

JOHN BROWNE

THE *Annals of Loch Cé* state that Master John Browne, Sheriff of Mayo, set out in 1589 with a force of three hundred men to plunder Erris and that he committed many depredations and homicides. This Browne was the ancestor of the Brownes of Westport, the Neale and Breaffy. He reached Carrigahowley Castle on the 7th February, where he was told he was not welcome. But he kept on, marching by the way the Four Masters call Bealach an Diothruibh (the Desert Road). Here he was intercepted by the Burkes, and in a close fight his soldiers were routed and he himself beheaded. The place of his death we identify with Lag a' Bhrúnaigh (Browne's Hollow), near the Leap at Furnace. The then usual way to Erris from Carrigahowley was by Furnace, Shramore and Mám a' Rata. Even today most of the district is a desert.

PARSON GOULDSMITH

IN a deposition dated 30th December, 1643 (T.C.D. F.3.2), John Gouldsmith, Parson of Brashoole, Co. Mayo, swore he was formerly a "Romish Papist," that his brother, a priest in Antwerp, wrote him a letter advising him to leave Burrishoole for the sake of his wife and children, that the bearer of the letter was Fr. Richard Barret, a Jesuit and an agent for the Irish. Gouldsmith further says that he was attacked in his house at midnight in 1641 and robbed of all his goods, worth £500, and expelled from his church, his lands and his living worth £100 per annum "whereof since he hath lost two years' profits," that one Edmund Ó Maley McLoughlin would have cut out his tongue, "for which purpose he came there," had not a friar begged for him on his knees. Others he accuses are Hugh Óge McCane of Castleaffy, gent., Tibbot Kelly of Balyveaghan, Edmund Óge of Rosnafrare (Ros na mBráthar) and Turlough Reogh. The last named was probably the McDonnell who had Drumbrastle in 1641. The names McCane and Magaen are identical. Hugh Óge was almost certainly a brother or a near relation of Honoria Magaen, martyred in 1653. "Papist" in "Romish Papist" above may be an error for "priest." Local tradition says that John Gouldsmith was a pervert priest.

CROMWELL

ONE night sometime after February, 1653, an English ship anchored off Melcomb Point. Next morning it sailed out Clew Bay with a full cargo - a cargo of slaves. The slaves were men, women and children of the parish who had been seized at random by the savage Cromwellian soldiery and driven at the point of the bayonet, on board ship. As elsewhere in Ireland, no mercy was shown, no human tie regarded. Children were torn from their mothers' arms, husbands were dragged from their weeping wives, young men and girls were rounded up like so many cattle. Slaves were needed for the plantations of the West Indies and Cromwell would supply the need. How many were taken away on that occasion we do not know. The horror of that night lives on in the memory of the people. It was a night of woe, filled with the cries and lamentations of the terrified captives, answered by the despairing weeping of their heartbroken relatives and neighbours. The tradition is that they were kept till daylight in an old house at Melcomb and then put on board the slave ship. They sailed with the tide into the unknown. After that, all is silence.

CATHOLIC RELIEF ACTS

UNDER the Penal Laws the Irish Catholic was an outlaw. In 1759, the Lord Chancellor laid down "that the laws of this land did not presume that an Irish Papist existed in the Kingdom, nor could they breathe here without the connivance of the Government." But by 1778 there was some change in outlook, no doubt induced by the victories of the American Revolutionaries. By an Act of that year Catholics were allowed to hold, inherit and transmit land in the same way as Protestants, provided they took the oath of Allegiance. In 1782, Catholics could erect their own schools if the Protestant bishop permitted; they could own a horse worth more than £5; they could assist at Mass without being compelled to inform on the priest. In 1793, they could vote at elections, but they could have no bells on their churches. The tenure of land became entirely unrestricted. These "privileges" could not be availed of unless the Qualification Oath of Allegiance to the English King was taken. A number of Burrishoole people took the oath in July, 1793, and so could vote. They are from many villages but most of the names have Newport as address of convenience. It is of interest to find that some of those who took the oath had no scruples about joining the French five years later.

18th CENTURY MONUMENTS IN BURRISHOOLE

WE have only one tomb of the 17th century, that of David Óg O'Kelly, dated 1623, with inscription in Latin: *Orate pro anima Davidis oge Kelly qui me fieri fecit sibi et heredibus suis Anno Dni. 1623 et eius uxoris Anabla Barrett* - Pray for the soul of David Óg Kelly who had me made for himself and his heirs A.D. 1623 and (for the soul) of his wife Anabla Barrett). The next monumental slab in order of time is that of Daniel O'Donnell, dated 1736. The inscription is in English. From then on to our own times the language is always English. Yet in the 18th century the people were all Irish-speaking and knew little or no English. It was not love of English that influenced our forefathers. As all Catholic schools were forbidden the result was that very few, if any, could write Irish. The sculptors found it possible to learn enough English lettering for the purpose and there was no choice. It was English or nothing. In the list below, the year after the name is the year of death.

John Bourke, 1797; Constant Cleary, 1787; Macara Fergus, 1784; Patrick Gibbons, 1771; Loughlin Grady, 1790; Mary Joyce *(al.* Greaven), 1800; Honor Kilroy, 1790; John Kine, 1788 (Carrowsallagh); Owen Lavelle, 1788; Honoria Lunn, 1800; Patrick MacDanaugh, 1791 (ancestor of J. Gannon, J. Gallagher, Jim O'Donnell); Daniel McCain, 1788; Bridget Nelis, 1782; Patt O'Maley, 1792; Owen O'Malley, 1789; Mrs. Margaret O'Malley *(al.* Tasbroch), 1789; Dennis Sweeney, 1789; Bridget *(al.* Mulloy), wife of Dennis, 1786; their son, Fr. Manus, 1799, aged 36. Cucogry O'Cleary, one of the Four Masters, may have been buried in Burrishoole. His will, dated 8th Feb., 1664, mentions the abbey. The name Macara is still in the Fergus family. It appears to have been an O'Kelly name, the original of which is Macarius.

In Killeen, Tíranáir, there are only a few 18th century slabs: Patrick Carolan, 1791; Teady Greaghan, 1796; Sarah Meehan, 1798 (relation of the late John Curran); Michael O'Donnell, 1799, ancestor of the O'Donnells of

Mulranny and of Martin O'Donnell of Kilmeena. Another slab has the following verse:

Remember, friend, as you pass by,
As you are now so once was I.
As I am now so you shall be,
Remember, friend, and think of me.

There are some Protestant graves in Cúl le Gréin: Kinning, 1796, and a number of Larminies, including Samuel, who swore against Fr. Manus, and in Knockavilly Glebe: John Wilks, weaver, 1789, and the Moores in the Moore vault, 1766.

THE ULSTER REFUGEES

IN Ulster, the Peep o' Day Boys and other secret Protestant societies were making life intolerable for their Catholic neighbours. No Catholic household was safe from those raiders of the night. The Government looked calmly on while Catholic homes went up in flames. The final blow was the "Battle of the Diamond" in Armagh, 21st September, 1795, when 20 or 30 Catholic defenders were killed. Thousands of harmless Catholics had to fly for their lives, leaving everything behind. Some 4,000 refugees poured into the baronies of Murrisk and Burrishoole. Lord Altamont, writing to Under Secretary Cooke on 27th July, 1796, says:

"Emigration from the North country continues. Many of them have fled, deprived of the principal part of their substance. A dangerous situation may arise unless the government comes to their aid at once. I fear emissaries of sedition have come, too … I am worried about little prints of the Crucifixion, with a ladder added to it, and tied up with little blue ribbons. I lately examined a priest who told me that these are called scapulars and used for devotional purposes, but I do not find this account satisfactory."

By the 27th November, when he writes again, the noble lord is more at ease but still very watchful. The scapular no longer scares him and, anyway, his brother, Denis Browne, has taken things in hand. Denis had got 4,000 of the refugees listed. "All have conducted themselves peaceably; I have the most positive assurances from the priests that intimation will be given if any ill intentions should be found among them." Enclosed with this letter was a list of fugitives who had come to "Newportpratt, Parish of Broussoul, Co. Mayo."

From Tyrone had come Philip Doyle, Owen Conlon, Patrick Devlin, Daniel O'Neill, Ed. McCray, Dan McSkinnador, Arthur McGurk, Hugh McTague, Hugh McGeoughagan, all with their wives and children; from Armagh are listed Robert Dwyer, William Mortimer, John Browne, Wm. McConville, Thomas Flinn, Patrick Makkin, Patrick Corrigan, Michael

Joyce, Michael Garrety, Daniel Gallagher, with their wives and children; from Down: Timothy Lennon and Hugh McConwell. Out of a total of 116 there were 78 children. But this list is not exhaustive. There were very many more. It is not possible to say whether those northerners are related to those of like name in the parish today.

BURRISHOOLE PORT

EVEN before the Normans appeared on the scene during the 13th century, Burrishoole, then named Ceann Tráchta, was a port of some importance. The invaders saw its possibilities and proceeded at once to build a town there, with a castle to guard it. The town flourished and for a long period was the chief port of Clew Bay. Italian maps of the 14th and 15th centuries clearly indicate that in those days Clew Bay was a busy commercial centre, carrying far more trade than the Bay of Galway. Those old maps refer to our bay as the *Lacus Fortunatus,* the Happy Lake, and to its islands as the *Insulae Fortunatae,* the Happy Isles. Burrishoole retained its leading position as a port down to the beginning of the 18th century. What form its commerce took we do not know. Malbie writing in 1580, speaks of the produce of the district and mentions great trees, grey marble and "plentiful commodities of every kind," as well as a "plentiful iron mine." In 1666, George Browne of the Neale reports on this mine and its smelting furnace as being in full operation, the products being exported. It is from this smelting furnace the village of Furnace got its present name. It was formerly Cnoc an Iubhair. Extensive remains of old buildings are still to be seen in the vicinity of the Mill Race. Where the mine was is not known, but we do know that the big woods that covered the surrounding area were cut down to the last tree to feed the furnace. In 1580, Malbie reported that it was proposed to make Burrishoole a walled town. Nothing, however, was done.

The population of the parish during those centuries must have been very small. As to the living conditions of the ordinary people we are almost entirely in the dark. There are references here and there to periodic famines and to hard times in general. But Irish law was still in full force and guaranteed security for every land-holder. Unlike English landlords, the Irish chiefs were not the owners of the territory they ruled, and the ordinary folk had their clearly defined rights and privileges, of which no chief could deprive them.

It seems certain that the great majority of the houses were of timber. The woods were everywhere and as yet it was not a crime to cut a tree. The monastery of Burrishoole was at first a timber structure.

Whatever little comfort there was in our countryside disappeared in the Cromwellian period. The 10 years from 1650 to 1660 must have been the most terrible in Irish history. Cromwell's savage troopers swept the land, plundering and burning and slaying. In their wake came plague and famine. Five-sixths of the people of Ireland perished, so that it is estimated that when Cromwell's work was done the population of the country was only half a million. Women and children died of starvation. Poor orphans driven from their homes were devoured in scores by the wolves. A man might travel 20 or 30 miles and not see a living creature. Man, beast and bird were all dead (Prendergast: *Cromwell. Settlement* 307). Our parish must have been almost depopulated. The plague struck here as elsewhere. In ministering to the poor victims, one of the friars of the abbey contracted the disease and died. To crown all, the Loughrea Commissioners were ordered to allow no Irish to settle in the county of Mayo, either as proprietors or tenants, to the end that it should be planted with English (Prendergast, op.cit. 163).

But by the grace of God a remnant of our people survived and, when Cromwell was gone to his account, they had begun once more to increase and multiply. But they had now dwelling in their midst many Catholics from Ulster who had been driven westwards. These Ulstermen had come in their hundreds, especially from Donegal, Derry and Tyrone. In the beginning they were looked on by some as little better than raiders and robbers, *na hUltaigh bhradacha* as they were called. The men of Tíranáir, miserable as their condition was, were, as they have ever been, men of spirit. They took the Ulstermen in hand and at the bridge of Bellacragher, near Mulranny, taught them a lesson they never forgot. A few years later, we find the men from the North settled in peace here and there in the district.

The coming of Pratt, former Treasury official, shortly after 1700, was the beginning of the end for Burrishoole as a port and a market. This gentleman conceived the grandiose idea of building a new town on a different site. In this he succeeded, although in the process he beggared himself and departed a bankrupt. All the reward he got was that the town was called, after him, Newport-Pratt. By 1752, the parochial market was well established on the new site. Writing that year, Pococke says in his Tour: "The market of Newport consists chiefly of frieze, yarn, stockings and different sorts of corn. Provisions are very cheap from June to Christmas, beef a penny, mutton 5 farthings a pound, chickens pence a piece, a fat goose for sixpence, a turkey for the same, and fat ducks two pence a piece. Fish is also very cheap. Good wine £16 a hogshead ... On the 8th August, several people joined us going to the fair of Balyheane, and we made up a caravan of 17 horses. We stopped twice and I divided my liquor among them and to the two or three Protestants my meat also." (P.95). At that time, Saturdays as well as Fridays were days of abstinence for Catholics. That 8th August was Saturday.

McParlan *(Statistical Survey of Mayo)* reports in 1801: "Habitations: some are very poor, made of turf sods, badly roofed, full of smoke, no chimneys. Since the commencement of separate tenures the cabins begin to improve, and a separate cowhouse and barn are often to be seen. Fuel is turf; food consists of potatoes, oaten bread, milk, flummery and, on the seacoast, fish. Men and women appear decently clothed on Sunday, generally in their own manufacture of friezes, flannels and druggets. Thick-sets, cottons, stuff, and baizes are often worn. 32 inch bandles of frieze cost 2/- to 2/4 each. 10 bandles make a suit. Add 4 yards of flannel as lining at 1/1 a yard, plus 3/- to the tailor. Total for a suit is £1 15 10d. Shoes are 5/6, a hat is 4/4, stockings are 1/1, an overcoat is 16/-. Total outfit thus costs £2 17 3d. The men wear an overcoat always, in winter for cold, in summer for show."

McParlan says the "Barony of Burrishoole exports yearly 150 tons of oats, 50 of barley and 100 tons of potatoes. Crops are rotated: first crop, potatoes; second, barley; third, oats and, fourth, after a fallow, flax. The common loy does nearly all the work. In the whole barony there are only five or six common ploughs. Harrows have only wooden pins. Very often a hand rake is used for harrowing. The turf slane is the only other implement.

Pádraig Ó Móráin and his first wife, Nora Chambers.

Pádraig Ó Móráin and his second wife, Mary Alice McFadden.

*Church of the Immaculate Conception, Mulranny,
erected in 1905 by Rev. Peter Varden, C.C. and
enlarged in 1930 by Very Rev. Canon MacDonald, P.P.*

*Pádraig Ó Móráin and Rev. Luke Taheny, O.P. at Furnace Leap,
Summer 1950.*

Pádraig Ó Móráin with Standing Stone, Ballycroy, July 1942.

His Grace, Most Rev. Dr. Walsh, Archbishop of Tuam, is a native of Burrishoole parish, a short history of which is contained in this book.

Pádraig Ó Móghráin

Comóradh Chéid a Bhreithe

FIDES NON TIMET

MORAN

*Cover of Booklet celebrating the centenary of the birth of
Pádraig Ó Móráin in 1986.*

PÁDRAIG Ó MÓRÁIN
(1886-1966)

No green food is used in winter. Cattle are of the old bad breed. This is not a cattle-feeding country. The only stock are those of the poor, fed in the houses in winter. There are no hides or tallow worth mentioning and only enough wool to clothe the people themselves. Every villager has a working garran (horse), and about six acres of green, usually reclaimed land. Fences are very bad. The manures used are black mud and sand and lime mixed, seaweed and sometimes limestone gravel.

"Numbers of people used to take farms in conjunction and build houses in clusters. Only very lately did this partnership begin to dissolve. Now they are beginning to subdivide the farms and take any leases they can get separately. But the houses are still very little detached."

This "partnership" was necessitated by the poverty of the people. The gracious English queen, Elizabeth, deprived them of all rights to the lands they had held from time immemorial and "granted" their property to greedy land-grabbers, like the Earl of Ormond. Half a century later, as a result of the Cromwellian tyranny, the poverty of the ordinary people was indescribable. They were so impoverished that none could dream of taking a holding of land on his own. The only solution was for a number of people to take such a holding in partnership, one or two of them being nominated as the legal tenant. The others paid their share of the rent to such nominated person and he paid the landlord. This is the class of tenant George Browne means when he says that nearly all the Burrishoole tenants were Ulstermen. If we took his words at their face value we could only conclude that all the old stock had disappeared. The Ulstermen had been able to bring a good deal of their cattle with them and were, accordingly, in a better position than the impoverished natives, and as such were, naturally, selected to be named as tenants on the rent roll. Having taken over the farm, the partners divided it, each getting a share of the good land and the bad land, a piece here and a piece there. When in 1793 it became possible for Catholic tenants to obtain leases, the partnerships began to dissolve. Many took out leases for the plots they held themselves and became independent tenants, thus creating the rundale system, which even still persists in places. Striping by the Land

Commission has, however, practically eliminated it.

In addition to paying rent, the tenants had also to pay tithes to the Protestant minister. McParlan says that the Catholic tenants had to give the minister every year a tenth of their corn or its value, a tenth of their hay and even one sheep out of every ten they had. In Burrishoole parish, unlike other districts, the minister did not collect marriage money, christening money, couple money or other small things of that kind. Potatoes also were free.

McParlan notes that "every cabin has a loom. They spin and weave pieces of linen for the Castlebar and Westport markets... There are now in Newport upwards of a hundred girls employed in a straw hat manufactory. The bonnets or hats made there are sold from 4/- to 26/- each. Very small girls earn 6d. to 15d. per day. People wear the hats, not for charity, but for their fineness and excellence."

Patrick Lynch tells of his journey from Bangor to Newport across the mountains. He got to Strath-Fairne (Srath Fearna, now Shramore) in the evening of 22nd May, 1802: "There are but few huts here. I crossed the moor to a cabin of stone, the best looking of them. I got a drink, gave tobacco and took a smoke. The house is full of kids. Got into Newport about nine. I got a good bed. Breakfast was ditto. Got Mass at one o'clock. Set off for Castlebar." (Fox: *Annals of Irish Harpers,* 1911).

THE LAND

THE constant bickering and fighting amongst the Irish nobility in Connacht in the 13th century enabled the Butlers to seize and hold large tracts of land in Burrishoole. Their grip was broken in 1272 but it was only to allow another horde of English invaders to replace them. These latter, the de Burgos, turned in time fully Irish. They adopted all the Irish customs and made the Irish language their own. For 300 years they ruled undisturbed. It must have come as a rude shock when they discovered in the 16th century that the Umhall they had held so long was not, after all, their property but belonged, by order of Elizabeth, to Thomas Dubh Butler, Earl of Ormond. The rapacious earl thought it title enough for him that 300 years earlier his family had claimed to be "Lords of Akyll and Owyll." Elizabeth's document confirmed possession to Ormond of all the de Burgo lands, some 5,000 acres, and all their castles (*Galway Arch. Jour.* XVI 139). On the 16th June, 1612, James 1 set out in detail the Burrishoole holdings of the noble Butler. These two documents only sanction Butler's claim. He was already in possession. In 1594 we find Tióbóid na Long, son of the great chief, Richard an Iarainn and Gráinne Ní Mháille, as a mere tenant, paying rent to Ormond. In 1617, Tióbóid held lands in Tíranáir. In 1636, the only Burkes holding any land in the parish were Miles Burke, Lord Mayo, son of Tióbóid, in Keelogues and Ardagh, and David Burke in Ardagh and Roslynagh.

As the Burkes leave the stage, another family, the O'Kellys, step on. They were of that branch of the O'Kellys of Hy Many who had settled in Carra about 1500 and built the castle of Donamona. They had removed to Burrishoole by 1623. David Óg O'Kelly erected a monument in the abbey in that year. The Strafford Inquisition of 1636 lists seven of the name as owning land in Roskeen, Rosgalive, Doughil, Sandhill, Lettermoghera and several of the islands. In 1641, fourteen members of the family held 1400 acres of profitable land in the parish. In 1653 Cromwell dispossessed them.

The Cromwellians left the Ormond estate untouched. The lands held by the O'Kellys and other lands in the parish were confiscated. Lord Baltinglass was deprived of his big estates in Leinster and given 400 acres in Burrishoole. Lord Ikerrin got 1400 acres in Umhall as compensation for the large property he had been robbed of elsewhere. Lord Mayo also got some land. Ormond's agent was Sir John Browne of The Neale. John's son, George, visited Burrishoole in 1665 and wrote back a very interesting letter to his father. In it he says that the tenants on Ormond's lands are mostly Ulstermen "and those always uncertain" in the matter of rent. "It were a discredit to you that his Grace's rent should be lessened during your time. You write of hopes that my Lord (Ormond) would have those lands of my Lord Ikerrin. The land is so intermixed amongst his Grace's that it will be most inconvenient to be without it." (Ormond MSS. N.S. II 211, 212). But it was John Browne, son of Sir John, who bought the Ikerrin lands, and also Lord Mayo's lands in Tíranáir (Quit Rents 1676). John became bankrupt in 1698. His properties were listed for sale. The list shows he owned then the Ikerrin and much of the Mayo estate. In the sale the Knoxes and Gores bought Tíranáir. John retained the Loch Feagh portion of his property, that is, Lettermoghera, Treenbeg, Treenla and Glennamo. His Rent Roll of 1704 mentions a tenant there, Eneas MacDonnell, who owed £107 and would not pay. A note says: "I sent several times to distraine and always rescued." In course of time John's descendant, Lord Sligo, was landlord. A ruthless tyrant, he brooked no "rescue". In the famine years he evicted every one of his forty tenants in Treenbeg and mercilessly flung them out on the roadside to die. Thus was formed the Treenlar farm. A similar fate was in his mind for the poor people of Lettermoghera. By some chance, two of these tenants had leases, and their holdings, being in the centre of the village, blocked the efforts of the noble marquis to form yet another farm - the farm of Lettermoghera.

The Butlers held on till 1696. In that year, the Earl of Arran, grandson of the Duke of Ormond, leased the Burrishoole estate to Sir Henry Bingham for 31 years and at the same time leased it "in reversion" to Thomas Medlicote for 999 years. This lease to Medlicote was equivalent to a complete sale and brought to an end Butler ownership in Burrishoole. The Binghams paid no rent and Medlicote evicted them in 1719, (Bingham Deeds 141 P.R.O.). On Bingham's eviction, a Mr. Pratt, who was clerk of the Treasury got a lease of the estate from Medlicote. He became insolvent and Medlicote ejected him. Part of the property was sold in 1774 to John Browne, Earl of Altamont. There was some huggermugger on Browne's part and the lands fell back to Medlicote, who in 1785 finally sold the entire estate to Sir Neal O'Donnell for the huge sum of £33,598 19 4d.

CLANN DÁLAIGH

THE O'Donnells (Clann Dálaigh) of Newport were the lineal descendants of Niall Garbh O'Donnell of Donegal, cousin to Red Hugh. Niall had himself made chief of his name in 1602 on the death of Red Hugh in Spain. He is not one of our national heroes. He dealt rather in treachery and did not hesitate to join the English against his own countrymen. He was rewarded for his services in the characteristic English way. He was lodged in the Tower of London in 1608. There he died a miserable death in 1626. His son, Manus, a colonel in Owen Roe O'Neill's army, was killed at the battle of Benburb in 1646. Manus's son, Rory of Lifford, was the first of the family to settle in Mayo. Rory's son, Manus (Col. Maney), fought at Limerick in 1691 in the army of King James. He was admitted to the benefit of the famous Treaty. He is the first of the O'Donnells who is mentioned as of Newport, Co. Mayo, though his first residence appears to have been at Rosturk. When Col. John Browne drew up his rent roll in 1704, it was found that, though Manus had had the fishing of the Burrishoole and Rosgalive rivers for many years, he had never paid rent. He claimed he had never been put in possession of the fishing. Under the Registration Act of 1704, he went surety for several priests in the sum of £50 each. He died in 1736.

Manus left three sons, Charles Roe, the eldest, Manus, and Hugh the youngest. Hugh appears to have lived at Melcombe near Newport. Melcombe is a placename imported by the Binghams, whose English home was Melcombe Bingham in Dorsetshire. Hugh gave £10 towards the erection of a Catholic church in Newport in 1750. Pococke met him in 1752. He died in 1762.

Hugh's son, Neal, "bent upon the winning," took steps at once to secure his worldly position. On the 14th November, 1763, scarcely a year after his father's death, he solemnly renounced the faith of his fathers and became a Protestant. His uncle, Manus, followed his example on 27th September, 1766, and died the following year. One of Manus's seven daughters, Elinor, who afterwards married the notorious duelist, Caesar French, joined her father and her cousin in 1766.

With the change over to Protestantism, the way to advancement was wide open to this scion of the princely family of O'Donnell. By 1768 he was a magistrate. In December, 1780, he was created a baronet. Before the end of 1780 he had bought for £20,000 the lands of the former Abbey of Cong. Five years later he became owner of the Medlicott Burrishoole estate at a cost of £33,598 19 4d. Where did the money come from? Neal's contemporaries were apparently as puzzled as we are, as we can see from the curious statement made by Rev. Mr. Benton in 1800. Benton stated: "The family hold in this country, from the fortuitous acquisition of property, no inconsiderable rank."

Pocoke says that in 1752 the Medlicott estate yielded only £1,700 a year. But in 1800 Sir Neal's income was £8,000 a year (evidence of Rev. MP. Heron at the 1800 inquiry). Whatever may be said about that, O'Donnell does not appear to have been a harsh landlord. There are traditions that portray him as a genial, kindly man, very fond of a wager. Although now a Protestant, he sent his children, according to the old Irish custom, to be fostered in the homes of his tenants, as he himself had been fostered in a lowly house in Ballycroy. Nor did the custom die with him. We find that even his grandson, Sir Richard, who died in 1879, was a foster-child of the O'Donnell family of Rossmore. Neal was captain of the Newport Company of Volunteers in 1782. He was a contemptible figure in the '98 struggle. His treatment of Fr. Manus Sweeney was deplorable, but what stands above all to his eternal discredit is the vindictiveness of the evidence he so willingly gave at the court martial where the poor priest was being tried for his life. Some would think that he redeemed himself somewhat by his uncompromising opposition to the Union. He died in January, 1811.

Sir Neal had four sons and two daughters. The two eldest sons, Hugh and James Moore, predeceased him. Neal, the third son, was his successor. Connell, the youngest, died childless some time in the eighteen-forties. The daughters were Margaret, who married Sir Capel Molyneux, and Maria, who married Dodwell Browne of Rahins. Hugh was an officer in the English army and, as we know, "flew from Kerry" to fight the "rebels in rags" at Ballinamuck. He and his brother, James Moore, were members of Grattan's Parliament. Their father had bought for them the "rotten boroughs" of Ratoath and Donegal. When the proposals for the Union came up for discussion in College Green, the two brothers, backed by their family in Newport, vehemently opposed them. In a maiden speech in the Irish House of Commons, on the 22nd of January, 1799, Col. Hugh O'Donnell declared:

"Should the legislative independence of Ireland be voted away by a Parliament which is not competent thereto, I shall hold myself discharged from my allegiance (cry of "Order, order") . . . I will oppose the rebels in rich clothes with as much energy as I have ever done the rebels in rags … If my opposition to it in this House shall not be successful, I will oppose it in the field!" (Barrington, *Historic Memoirs* II 413, 415) The Colonel was not put to the test. For this speech he was dismissed from the army. He died the following September. The attitude of Hugh and his family greatly annoyed the smug old Marquis of Sligo. In a letter dated 26th May, 1799, the noble lord writes: "The O'Donels and General Trench are the only persons that openly take part against us (in the matter of the proposals for the Union), but we have some neutrals. The conduct of the O'Donels in the country has so lowered them with every gentleman, every loyal man in it, that they can do no prejudice whatever, and General Trench has no weight but that of his situation." (State Paper Office.)

James Moore O'Donel, Neal's second son, is a puzzle to us, as he was to the men of his time. After the defeat of the '98 Insurgents, he arrested scores of rebels and then, when they came up for trial, went to extraordinary lengths to defend them and save them from the gallows. He met his death at the hands of Major Denis Bingham on the 14th September, 1806, in a duel fought at Killanley Glebe, near Enniscrone in Co. Sligo. In the flamboyant inscription on his memorial tablet m Newport Protestant church, we read: "In arduous times he proved his loyalty to his king, in corrupt ones he supported the independence of his country, and as he lived a Man of Honour, so he died a Man of Courage in the 36th year of his age."

The second Sir Neal, known generally, as Neal Beg, is "the great little man" of Fr. Burke's reputed sermon. In his contest with the priest, he avers himself a strong Protestant. He was, however, no bigot. He justly boasts of his "sincere attachment to the Catholic Cause . . . and my services, weak but unwearied, under a Grattan, a Fingal and a Plunket." He says his father had given upwards of £300 to the Catholic chapel. He had, himself, given his mite, £100, and he would give more. But his interest was excessive and became interference, culminating in the ludicrous spectacle of the Protestant "lord of the soil" haranguing a Catholic congregation in their own church at the sacred hour of Mass. Fr. Bourke certainly taught him his place. The only reference to Neal Beg in the '98 period is that he fought at Ballinamuck under Cornwallis as captain of the Louth Militia (1800 Inquiry). He died 1st March, 1827.

Of Neal's children we have record only of Hugh James Moore, the eldest; Richard, the second son, and Mary, the eldest daughter. Hugh succeeded his father but his reign was short. On the 29th July, 1828, he met his death in Newport House in a shooting incident, whether accident, suicide or worse is not known. Richard became Sir Richard. Mary became a Catholic and entered the Presentation Convent in Galway on the 5th February, 1829. After a life of labour and prayer Sr. Mary de Pazzi O'Donnell died 12th November, 1864. In a letter which she sent to her relative, Le Conte Maurice O'Donnell of Austria, on 26th July, 1850, she appeals for help for her 900 poor children: "We are more alarmed for them now than when suffering the horrors of famine, or yet during the terrors of the cholera, for the present plague is far more frightful, namely, the most wild set of mad, false preachers that ever visited an unhappy island - poor, suffering Ireland. They have plenty of money, they are bribing all, but what they most wish to get is our poor children."

Sir Richard married, in 1831, Mary, daughter of George Clendining of Westport. Clendining was a banker. He fixed his Mary's dowry at her weight in gold. Mary improved "the shining hour" by concealing two smoothing irons in her bosom when she was being weighed. We are reminded that when Rory O'Donnell of Lifford was married his wife's dowry was also her weight in gold. Rory's wife was Margaret Sheile, a farmer's daughter. "Notwithstanding the gold, the O'Donnells felt their pride humbled by such a marriage and some of them prevailed on Rory to abandon his wife, to whom he was lawfully joined in the hallowed bands of matrimony by one of the friars of Burrishoole." *(Ord. Survey Letters:* Mayo I, p. 173). Sir Richard needed the money badly. His estate was heavily mortgaged. The whole family had been borrowing money, and continued borrowing and selling till nothing was left but the shadow of their former greatness. The Clendinings were soon in bankruptcy and Sir Richard was involved. He was forced to sell his Cong estate and large portions of his Burrishoole land, too. Even then, he could not pay his debts.

In spite of his debts and in spite of the drink and dissipation that was making his house a den of infamy, Sir Richard set himself forth as a wondrously religious man. O'Donovan begins the O'Donnell pedigree thus: "Sir Richard, the Darbyite or swaddling preacher, son of Neal, etc." The Darbyites were founded in Dublin in 1830 by John Nelson Darby, a Dublin lawyer, who became a Protestant minister but seceded. He is regarded as the founder of the Plymouth Brethren. It did not take Sir Richard long to "ketch on" as the Americans would say. O'Donovan wrote his account of him in 1838. The noble baronet built for his sect a conventicle, where he himself was preacher and minister and bishop, all rolled together. The conventicle is now the Catholic parochial hall. More wonderful still, Sir Richard taught school. "Sir Richard O'Donel and his lady have established schools on liberal principles. The lady herself teaches two or three days in the week and Sir Richard himself has an admirably well-fitted schoolroom, where he teaches a Sabbath school himself." (Mrs. Asenath Nicholson: *Ireland's Welcome to the Stranger,* New York, 1847.)

The "liberal principles" of his school were not applicable to O'Donnell's Catholic tenants. Of Catholicism and of everyone and everything connected with it he appears to have had an insane hatred. Woe

64

to the Catholic who aroused his anger. It was the day of the petty tyrant, and the great man roamed his domain with a horse-whip ever ready and often mercilessly used (in reality he was in stature little more than a dwarf). The law of the land was behind him. With Nangle of Achill he co-operated to the full.

The "colonies" of Bible-readers and "soupers" who set up in Kilbride and other places to bring to the poor Papists the light of the Gospel came with his blessing. He helped the good work by evicting every Catholic family he could. His policy was extermination. But when all was over the only family exterminated was his own. The broad acres that were once Sir Richard's are now occupied and owned by Catholic families, many of whom are the descendants of those whom he cruelly cast out to die on the roadside or in the workhouse. Of the O'Donnell line nothing remains but the bones that are mouldering in the family vaults.

Sir Richard died in 1879. Sir George, who succeeds him, appears to have taken little interest in religion. Even in his father's lifetime, he married a Catholic, Mary Kirwan of Bawn House, Co. Longford. She predeceased him. She lived and died a Catholic and is buried with her mother, Louisa Kirwan, in the tomb in the Catholic church grounds. It was, no doubt, due to her that the Sisters of Mercy secured the site on Barrack Hill for their convent and schools. She also donated the two fine stained-glass windows in the Convent chapel. Sir George died childless in 1889. The property fell to his niece, Millicent. She married Edwin Thomas, who assumed the name O'Donel. Their son, George, was killed in France in June, 1915. He was married but had no children. His wife auctioned everything off. The house and garden passed to Mr. Michael McShane who, in turn, sold them to the late Mr. Mumford-Smith. Now Newport House, once the residence of the O'Donnells, has become Newport House Hotel. *Sic transit gloria mundi.* The O'Donnells of Newport have gone and their place knows them no more.

THE CATHACH

THE *Cathach* is a manuscript written by the hand of St. Columcille himself. It contains about half of the Book of Psalms. It was called the *Cathach,* or "Battler," because in the old times the O'Donnells used to carry it with them to battle. Cathbarr Ó Domhnaill, who died in 1106, got made for it a case or shrine of silver overlaid in parts with gold. The shrine was repaired several times. The present lid is of the 14th century. Daniel O'Donel, who fought at Limerick in 1691, took it to France. In 1723, he enclosed it in a silver box and left it in a monastery with instructions that it was to be handed over to whoever should prove himself chief of the O'Donnells. (Lawlor: *Proceedings R.I.A.* 1916. vol. XXXIII.) Lawlor says the shrine was discovered in Paris by Sir Capel Molyneux and delivered by him to his father-in-law, Sir Neal O'Donnell, in 1802. Sir Neal had got from Sir William Betham, assistant to the Ulster King-at-Arms, a certificate stating that he, Sir Neal, was chief of the O'Donnells. Petrie says it was Fr. Prendergast, Abbot of Cong, who found the shrine and it was to the second Sir Neal it was given. If Petrie is right, it is strange that it was Sir Neal Beg's mother who, in 1814, brought an action against Betham for opening the shrine. It was from her he had got the loan of it in 1813. It was an express condition of the loan that the shrine be left unopened. It was believed that the *pignus* or relic enclosed in it was a bone, or bones, of Columcille. Betham got curious. He saw a small hole and poked in a small wire. Hearing a noise like the rustling of paper, he succumbed to temptation, opened the case and found the manuscript.

Matthew O'Connor and others denounced Betham's certificate to Sir Neal as a falsehood and his pedigree of the O'Donnells as a fabrication. John O'Donovan, however, proved that the pedigree was historically correct. That did not mean that Sir Neal was the head of the family. By right of seniority, the *Cathach* should have gone to Lewis O'Donnell of Killeen, Co. Mayo. Lewis lived till 1822. His father, Charles Roe, was Col. Maney's eldest son. Hugh Mór, Neal's father, was the Colonel's youngest son. The O'Donnels of Larkfield, Co. Leitrim, claimed that they were the senior O'Donnells and that by right the *Cathach* was theirs. They claimed as being descendants of a younger brother of Niall Garbh. The shrine and its manuscript are now in the R.I. Academy.

"WHO FEARS TO SPEAK OF '98"

NEWPORT had its company of Volunteers in 1782, as we learn from the Memorial Tablet to Captain de Bille. In the '98 period, the fear of a French invasion had led to the formation of companies of cavalry in many districts. The Newport company - called the Newport-Pratt Cavalry - was under the command of James Moore O'Donnell, second son of Sir Neal, with his brother Connel as lieutenant, and John MacLaughlin of Newfield as cornet.

Nothing of note occurred in the parish till May 1797, when five men were arrested on suspicion of being United Irishmen and brought before James Moore O'Donel. Two of the five, Lennons from the North, escaped. Robert McDonnell, cooper, of Ballycastle, Henry Duffy, dealer, from the North, and a tailor, "X," were tried by James M. O'Donnell. "X" turned informer. He said he was coming from the Market House of Newport on the 10th May to warm his "Iron called a Goose." He met McDonnell and Thomas Gibbons of Rossakeeran near the chapel of Moina. One of them asked him: "Are you UP?" (Are you United Patriot?). He also said there was talk in Larminie's public house. A Protestant heard the talk and reported it but did not come to court. That is all the State papers contain. But that there was more is clear from the boast made later by O'Donnell that "previous to the landing of the French he took up four United Irishmen in Newport and, from their examination, discovered that John Gibbons, senior, of Westport, was secretary of the United Irishmen there." (Joly 1034, 26, Nat. Lib.). He sent the information to Denis Browne.

On the landing of the French in Killala in August, 1798, all the Catholic members of the Newport-Pratt Cavalry, with their Cornet, John MacLoughlin, and some Protestants, rushed to join them. In the Inquiry of 1800 (Joly ibid.), Rev. Mr. Benton testified: "Every Papist in the town of Newport-Pratt was a rebel in '98 . . . The town, the property and residence of Sir Neal O'Donel, was the sink of rebellion." Dr. Thomas Ellison said at the same inquiry that John Irwin had testified that "it would be endless work to name such inhabitants of the town as were concerned in the rebellion . . . that every Papist in the town was implicated more or less." Men of property, like the MacLaughlins of Newfield, John, Henry and Peter, and the O'Malleys of Burrishoole, Austin and Joseph, and Peter Gibbons, a rich Newport merchant, did not hesitate for a moment. With them to Killala went every man who could get a horse. The number of horses reported missing by their owners in Newport in those far off August days tells its own story. It was again "my kingdom for a horse" and even the parish priest's nag was found of use in the emergency of the hour. On the 27th August, 1798, Peter Gibbons returned to Newport after the "Races of Castlebar" with the French officer, Boudet, and in Main Street joyfully planted the "Tree of Liberty." When the storm broke, Sir Neal O'Donnell fled and did not feel safe till he found himself in the bosom of Cornwallis's English army. There he joined his son, Neal, captain of the Louth Militia, and his eldest son, Hugh, who "flew from Kerry" to help Cornwallis against the "rebels in rags." James Moore and his brother, Connell, are not accounted for.

On the 5th September, the Insurgents evacuated Newport. It was now safe for Sir Neal to return. He came back and claimed that with two men he had recaptured the town. He did not need even the two men. He could have taken the place on his own because there was not one left to oppose him. His first brave deed was to burn the "Tree of Liberty," his second to capture Fr. Manus Sweeney. Like a Knight of the Round Table charging in the lists, the noble baronet swept down on the defenceless priest and struck him savagely with his gun. The badly wounded priest was seized and bound with ropes and hauled to Newport House. When the Protestant minister, Rev. Josiah Heron, made clear to Sir Neal that his arrest of Fr. Sweeney might lead to regrettable consequences, he hastily released his prisoner.

The Inquiry held in Castlebar on 1st Dec., 1800, makes curious reading. The Rev. Benton had accused Capt. James M. O'Donel of helping the rebels in '98 and, at the Captain's demand, a Governmental inquiry was instituted. Having made the statement that every Papist in Newport was a rebel, Benton went on to say that the "Tree of Liberty" was planted by a member of the Newport Cavalry, a yeoman named Peter Gibbons. At Gibbons's courtmartial there were only two to give evidence in his defence. These two were Stephen Davis, Captain O'Donel's confidential friend, and John Rogers, clerk to the yeomanry corps, also a Protestant. Matthew Evans of Capavicar swore that James Jordan said "that Capt. O'Donel had been for about the last month or six weeks encouraging them to be United Irishmen." Anthony Wilks, who said he was an Orangeman, swore that Lt. O'Donel on one occasion, before the French came, heard James Wilks playing "The Protestant Boys" ("Croppies, Lie Down") on a fiddle and was so enraged that he rushed at Wilks and swore that that tune should never be played in Newport. Benton alleged that Lt. O'Donel had sworn his life against two of the Wilks because they had sworn information against James Kelly, yeoman, for being in the rebellion. "These men are very loyal," said Rev. Dean Browne (James Kelly was a foster-brother of O'Donel). James Anderson of the Tirawley Cavalry swore that Capt. O'Donel searched Peter Gibbons's house but that he was very reticent about the papers found there; that he found there a hat decorated with ribbons and remarked that the hat could go to hell, that the rascal had corresponded with the French Directory. Lt. O'Donel had released the rebel officer, Heavey, who had been captured in Tuam by Joseph Kenning, a Newport-Pratt yeoman. James Kelly, too, who had been deeply implicated, was allowed to escape. General Trench suggested dereliction of duty on the part of the O'Donels in releasing "priest Sweeney."

There were others, too, who were guilty but they were all let go scot-free. George Wilks swore that the following Newport-Pratt yeomen had deserted on the arrival of the French: Hugh O'Donel, Wm. Hill, Patrick Cunny, John Joyce, John Slattery, James Cannon, John Nixon, Patrick Gibbons, Edmund Hevron; that of these Patrick Gibbons, John Slattery and John Nixon were somehow back again in the Cavalry; that back, too, in the force was Edmund Hevron who had been actually tried as a rebel and sentenced to transportation. Other evidence was that Patrick Keane, Ned Burke and John McGuire were still members of the Cavalry Corps although all three had been in the rebellion.

In reply to the charges against them, the O'Donels set out to prove their loyalty. Capt. James recounted his exploits: he had before the coming of the French lodged Father Paul Feighan (Feehan) in gaol for seditious talk among the lower classes; he had taken up four United Irishmen in Newport in '97 and got information from them about John Gibbons of Westport, which information he had sent to the Hon. Denis Browne (a man better known later as "Soap the Rope"); he had sent in as prisoners for being concerned in the rebellion the following: Peter Gibbons, Richard Gibbons, Christopher Crump, Adam Gallagher, John McGuire, Anthony Daly, Patrick Keane, John Gannon, Ed. Garvey, John Kearney, John Kyle, John Clarke, Daniel Sweeney, Ed. Hevron and - Hamrogue; that he had lodged Hevron, Keane, Gannon and Hamrogue in Castlebar gaol on the information of A. Wilks; that he had in July, '99, arrested three men from Derrylohan - Denis McGuire, as a "rebel and horse-thief" (he had borrowed a horse to join the French), Hugh McGuire and Peter Duffy - all three being bound to the peace; he had searched Peter Gibbons's house and had said then that he would take Gibbons, if he were left to do it in his own way; he had searched Mr. O'Malley's house in Burrishoole from top to bottom for O'Malley's son, Austin, a rebel captain; he had allowed John Nixon to rejoin because the man said he was sorry and because of the good conduct of Nixon's two uncles; that he was against the playing of such tunes as "The Protestant Boys" or "Croppies, Lie Down," because they were provocative. Further, constant trouble arose from the fact that "Croppies, Lie Down," the Orange favourite, and "Up With The Green," the Catholic favourite, had the same air. The Captain asked General Trench: "Did not the Newport Cavalry on service under Lt O'Donel act with courage, fidelity and loyalty?" Trench replied: "I do not recollect that they were on actual service. I knew not one corps from another, but I think one half of the corps ought to be hung, for on that occasion they all behaved exceedingly ill."

Sir Neal also defended himself and his family. It was not out of pity he had released "priest Sweeney," but because he was convinced that "the consequences of detaining him would have been the sacrifice of the loyal inhabitants by the rebels and the destruction of the town of Newport." He had himself recaptured the place with the aid of two men; he had prosecuted several rebels to conviction; he had gone at once to General Cornwallis and his two sons, Hugh and Neal, had fought against the insurgents at Ballinamuck. "The Court must hold," said Sir Neal, "that my sons and I are loyal subjects of the king." And so the Court held.

On the suppression of the rebellion, the hangman got into action. "English official records state that of the five hundred taken prisoners and tried by courtmartial one hundred were hanged." (Hayes: *Last Invasion Of Ireland. 179*). Many more were hanged without any trial. From the Newport area we find only three recorded as having been sentenced to death by courtmartial, Fr. Manus Sweeney, Peter Gibbons and his brother, Richard. Fr. Manus was the only one executed. He was hanged in Newport on the 8th June, 1799. There is a tradition that John McGuire of Derryloughan was hanged in Castlebar. There is no doubt that Austin O'Malley, James Kelly and several others would also have graced the gallows-tree had they been caught.

The sentence of death on Peter Gibbons was confirmed on the 30th April, 1799. But, as Benton said, "Gibbons effected out of prison his escape." Peter's wife, a sister of John MacLoughlin of Newfield, Tíranáir, was permitted to visit him in his cell. They exchanged clothes and Peter, as Mrs. Gibbons, walked out unmolested. He got away safely to America. His brother, Richard, was also sentenced to death but the Lord Lieutenant mitigated the sentence to transportation. Later he was a prisoner in England, where he died. The family to which these men belonged was not the Gibbons family of Mayo. They were descended from David FitzGibbon of Limerick, who had been transplanted by Cromwell to Inver, Erris, in 1653. Pat Gibbons of Newport who, about 1854, presented to the church the Perpetual Lamp which now hangs there, was the last of his race in Ireland (O'Hart's *Pedigrees,* Vol. II, New York, 1922).

There is no record whatever of the punishment inflicted on the

MacLoughlins of Newfield. We may be certain that they did not escape scot-free. The extremely prominent part they played in the Rising could hardly be overlooked. To Humbert in Ballina "from Mulranny arrived John McLoughlin of Tiernair with his three sons, one of whom, Peter, a student of Trinity College and a friend of Robert Emmet, had been expelled with him a few months before for patriotic activities." (Hayes op. cit. 62). Elsewhere, we are told that John McLoughlin led 250 men from Newport to Ballina. Rev. Josiah Heron testified at the O'Donel Inquiry, 1st Dec., 1800, that he had heard that Cornet MacLoughlin's brother had been expelled from the College of Dublin for being a member of the Assassination Committee and was later a leading rebel in Newport. Heron added that he himself had been taken by the rebels at Tíranáir and brought a prisoner to Newport, that he knew his captors, especially Peter and Henry McLoughlin and Joseph O'Malley (of Burrishoole). Mr. Heron was not an informer. His evidence was given when all was over. At the time, we feel sure that everyone expected to see John McLoughlin and his three sons hanged without mercy. But somehow they escaped that fate. It is likely that they were imprisoned for some time but, as far as we can judge, not for very long.

In the *Convert Rolls*, John McLoughlin, merchant, Newport, is recorded as having renounced the Catholic Faith in the Protestant church, Newport, on the 26th October, 1772. We know he did not persevere in his new religion. All his children were brought up Catholics. In 1810, at his own expense, he erected the Catholic church of Newfield. Hayes (op.cit.p.286) says: "In Tiernair Catholic church there is a holy water font with the inscription: 'Presented by John McLoughlin, 1810.'" This is incorrect. The inscription reads: "Erected by John McLaughlin, 1810." As well as being a merchant we find John in 1774 as tenant to Medlicott for big areas of land in Achill. When the fever-ridden Danish ship, Bornholm, was wrecked at Melcombe Point in March, 1782, John was kind to the stricken crew and it was in his house on Main St. that the master of the vessel, Captain de Bille, died. Whether de Bille rewarded his benefactor or not is a moot point. At any rate, it is true that the small house in which the Capt. died was that same year replaced by the big mansion that still stands, the present residence of Mrs. J. K. Moran. Some years later, John handed over the house and the business to his son-in-law, Peter Gibbons, and went himself to live as a country gentleman in Newfield House, Tíranáir. His position was that of under-landlord. How this system worked is shown in the case of Lord Sligo and the Evans lands. Sligo took over those lands, tenants and all, at a rent of £110. But like the publicans in the Gospel, he compelled the tenants to pay him the annual rent of £488, leaving him a net gain of £378. John McLoughlin was no tyrant, and he and his family appear to have been always on the most friendly terms with all their tenants. John died shortly after 1810 and was succeeded by his son, John, known locally as Seán Óg or Cian Óg.

Seán Óg is recorded as living at Newfield in 1837 (Lewis *Top. Dict.*). He was dead by 1839. In that year his son, Dominick, was master of New-field and his brother, Peter, of '98 fame, was living in Currane, Achill. The Famine brought ruin. "Income failed when the tenants fled from the scene in hunger. Members of the family sought to claim their shares and a whole series of Chancery cases followed, the costs being so great that when Baron Richards sold the holding there was little left for anyone." (J. F. Q., *Western People,* 23 Jan., 1954). The holding referred to was the Bunacurry estate in Achill, which Archbishop MacHale bought for the Franciscan Brothers in 1852. Gore failed to renew the Newfield lease and sold the lands to H. Smith of Louth. Dominick McLoughlin acted as Smith's agent for some time. In Griffith's *Valuation of 1855*, Dominick is named as owner of six houses in Newport but is not given as living at Newfield. It is likely that by then he had gone to America. Only the ruins of Newfield House remain. Its last occupant was the ill-fated James Hunter. Just as prominent as the McLoughlins in that short-lived fight for freedom were the O'Malleys of Burrishoole, Austin and his brother, Joseph. Hayes (op. cit. 159) says that Captain Joseph O'Malley of Burrishoole was hanged at Ballinamuck. That does not appear to be true. Joseph was one of those who arrested Rev. Mr. Heron and brought him a prisoner to Newport. Newport was then in the possession of the rebels but that possession lasted only one short week. On the 5th. September, the English were back. Ballinamuck was fought on the 8th September. It seems unlikely that Joseph O'Malley was present at the battle. Further, in the statement of claim made by Austin at the Mayo Assizes in 1836, he says that his brother, Joseph, died in 1804. Austin himself fought at Ballinamuck but he managed to escape and eventually made his way to France. In General Trench's list of wanted men he figures with £50 on his head. Miles Byrne (*Memoirs* II, 203) met Austin in Paris in 1803 and speaks of him in glowing terms. He was at that time a captain in the French Army. He served with distinction all through the Peninsular War in Spain.

On his return to France in 1812 he was suddenly struck blind and was forced to retire with a small pension. One of his two sons was promoted full colonel for bravery in the Crimean War and was placed in command of the 73rd Regiment. In 1805 Marsden wrote from Dublin Castle to Connel O'Donel telling him that Austin O'Malley was in Mayo and to see about him. But our brave Connel considered that discretion was the better part of valour and replied to Marsden that he and Sir Samuel O'Malley would have been glad to apprehend him but that it was not in their power, "there being no army here as the yeomanry are not on duty." (State Papers). Austin came back to Ireland in 1836 unmolested. He brought an action at the Mayo Assizes to recover from Mr. Martin Burke and Mr. Nixon that portion of his family's Carrowkeel lands designated Seafield and Old Furnace, with the fishery and the kelp shores. He himself received the greatest respect and courtesy but his claim was rejected under the Statute of Limitations. After the failure of his action, one tradition says he lived till his death in 1854 with Michael Coyne at Cahergal in the house that is now the residence of Mr. John Collins. Another tradition is that he was brought back to France by his son and died there.

Of the Sir Samuel O'Malley mentioned in Connel O'Donel's letter to Marsden nothing glorious can be recorded. O'Donovan gives his pedigree thus: "Owen, who shot his brother, son of Sir Samuel, who shot his mother, son of Owen Crosach (pockmarked), who died about 64 years ago, son of

George (who was the first of the family who played chess with spectacles Rabelais), son of Owen More, son of Emon Bacach, said to be a nephew of Gráinne." (Mayo Letters II, 13). But O'Donovan did not know everything. Owen Crosach, father of Sir Samuel, turned Protestant 12th January, 1757. He married twice. His second wife, Anne McGoeugh of Newry, was no better than she should have been, and grave doubt has been cast on the parentage of her son, Samuel. Owen died in the prison for debtors in Dublin in 1781. He was bankrupt. His body was left four days unclaimed in the filthy gaol. His wife was tried for poisoning him. The evidence against her was very strong but, being in some particulars incomplete, the verdict was acquittal (Sir Owen O'Malley: Family Letters). Though the father died a bankrupt, his son owned Clare Island. Some time after the Rebellion, Samuel seems to have called a public meeting in Castlebar for the purpose of organising the people of Mayo against all rebels and rebellious ideas. Lord Sligo was so pleased with the young man's loyalty that he persuaded the Government to make him a baronet. Thus at the age of 25 the son of Owen Crosach became Sir Samuel O'Malley. His line is long extinct.

THE 19th CENTURY

SMUGGLING appears to have been a very big industry in the first decades of the 19th century. The Revenue Police, who were in Newport in strength, established coastguard stations in Rossmore and Moynishmore in order to stop it. The chief of the smugglers was the famous Caiptín Seoirse Ó Máille. One of the Caiptín's ventures started on the 1st July, 1824, when he set sail for the Low Countries in his 27 ton boat *The Zephyr,* better known as *Slúipín Vaughan,* from its former owner. Associated with him were Matthew O'Kelly, Anthony O'Donnell and Owen Kelly, all of Newport. O'Donnell was with him on board. There were many others interested also, both Catholics and Protestants. *The Zephyr* returned around the north of Scotland. O'Donnell wanted to make for the Killeries where he knew big Jack Joyce (Jack na Báine) would welcome them. Captain Ó Máille would not agree. Instead, in spite of the great risk, he took his boat all the way to Carrigahowley. He sent word at once to John MacLoughlin of Newfield and to Matthew Gallagher of Newport. In a very short space of time the whole cargo - wines, tobacco, etc. - was disposed of. There was plenty of willing help. Captain Ó Máille then stripped the boat and had her almost scuttled when the Revenue Guards arrived. He had been once again too smart for them. One of the Guards who came too late was John Jackson, whose name is enshrined in Jackson's Hill at Newport. Some time later the Caiptín was kicked by a horse and was taken care of in the home of a namesake in Roskeen. In 1829 we find him building a boat in Newfield for John MacLoughlin. This was the boat called *The Brother and Sister,* after Dominic and Mary, John's children. By this time, the Caiptín's smuggling days were over. He died in the Workhouse in Westport. Lord rest his soul.

Rev. Mr. Nangle wrote a book, *The Origin, Progress and Difficulties of the Achill Mission.* In it, among other things, he tells that he had occasion to report to the Board of Education that James O'Donnell, master of Dugort school, had committed a crime, namely, that in a procession to meet

Archbishop MacHale he had carried a flag which bore the inscription: *Welcome Religion and Liberty.* The report is dated 8th September, 1835. Inspector James Kelly (nephew of Archbishop Kelly) investigated the matter and reported back to the Board that Nangle's charge was groundless. Nangle was not satisfied. He delved into O'Donnell's past. On the 13th July, 1836, he wrote again to the Board of Education: "I have been informed that O'Donnell was once in the Coastguard and was dismissed on account of being implicated in Ribbonism." The letter further charges that another factor in the dismissal was the use of seditious language by O'Donnell. All Nangle's efforts, however, were fruitless and O'Donnell was left undisturbed in his school in Dugort.

In speaking of *Ribbonism* Nangle had in mind what had happened in 1831. At that time, secret societies were rife, all going under the general name *Ribbonism.* There were White Boys, Steel Boys, Terry Alts and others. The penalty for membership of any of those bodies was transportation beyond the seas, usually to Van Diemen's Land (Tasmania). In October, 1831, a number of men from the parish were convicted of being *Steel Boys* and were transported. Among them was David Kelly of Newport, a brother of Fr. Walter Kelly. James O'Donnell, the schoolmaster, had been friendly with Kelly. Therein lay his crime. He had been a boatman in Lt. Irwin's Rossmore anti-smuggling guard. He had got that position through the influence of Sir Richard O'Donnell, to whom he was foster-brother. When Irwin heard he had been friendly with Kelly he dismissed him. Tradition says that Fr. Walter Kelly died of grief and shock soon after the sentence on his brother. Among the others transported were Edward and Thomas MacNally of Corrogaun and Bryce of Buckagh. The latter was the only one who returned. On the same occasion, Manus McDonnell of Bleachyard, a cousin of Fr. Manus Sweeney, was sentenced to 21 years transportation.

In 1836 the pier at Newport was built at the expense of the merchants of the town. In 1845 the eccentric American Protestant, Mrs. Asenath Nicholson, paid us a visit. This was on her way back from Achill, where she had gone to see the "wonderful" work Rev. Mr. Nangle was doing. She found nothing to praise there and said so. Neither did she altogether approve of the goings on at Newport fair on the 9th June. In Newport "I stopped at the house of Mr. Gibbon, the itinerant Bible Reader, and passed the time pleasantly with his family and the kind Christian widow, Arthur, who kept the post office. A kind of romantic charm seems flung about Newport." *(Ireland's Welcome to the Stranger.* New York, 1847).

Slater's Directory of Ireland, published in March 1846, is very informative. This lists one Catholic and three Protestant schools in Newport, and Catholic schools in Treenbeg and Deradda. The town Catholic school seems to be the present boys' school. It was a mixed school till the opening of the Convent school in 1887. The fact that in 1846 there were three Protestant schools in the place, combined with the presence in the town of two resident clergymen of the Established Church, a Presbyterian minister, and a Darbyite conventicle, indicates a considerable non-Catholic population. Even then, however, Protestants numbered only two or three percent of the teeming community. Today (1955) they represent not as much as one per cent. Slater says there were many shops in the town and that every need was catered for. A Richard Bird kept a hotel (where Kelly's garage now stands), and there were five inns or public houses. It was evidently a time of great prosperity. In 1841 the population of the parish was 11,942, of which 1,091 were in the town (census 1841). In 1846 the numbers had increased.

The life of the people in the pre-famine years appears to have been not altogether unhappy. Housing conditions were bad, but everywhere the old cabins built of sods of turf were being replaced by solid stone structures, roofed with bog-deal and thatched, with windows and chimneys. Dancing was a favourite pastime but it was strictly regulated. No late hours were tolerated. All had to be home not later than 10 o'clock so as to be in time for the family Rosary. The Rosary, with all its trimmings and the old traditional prayers, was a solemn function at which all were expected to be present. Then there was story-telling. There were scores of houses all through the parish where the people gathered to listen enthralled to the old tales told by masters of the craft. The listeners were transported out of their drab everyday existence and lived for the night in the heroic world of Fionn and Oscar and Oisín, of Goll Mac Morna and his ill-minded brother, Conan Maol, of Cúchulainn and the Knights of the Red Branch. These were mere childish tales. They were mighty stories told with dramatic art. Pádraig 'ac Aodhain (Pat Keane), the wonderful seanchaidhe of Murrevaugh, who died in 1926, could trace this tradition of storytelling back to 1750. Then we had our local poets. Some of these were exceedingly skilful but only odd verses of their work have come to us. The only complete piece we know of is *Rann an Mhadaidh,* composed before 1837 by Pádraig Mac a' Leá of Rosgalive.

This is a delightfully humorous account of a fanciful deer hunt. A version of this Rann was published in *Ar Aghaidh* of December, 1952, and succeeding months, but we have in the parish a longer and much better version. It should not be forgotten that at this period Irish was practically the only language spoken.

THE FAMINE

THE great famine of 1846 - 1848 soon put an end to this comparative prosperity. We have very little documentary evidence of the sufferings of our people in that hour of darkest tragedy. But the old people of fifty years ago who had seen the horrible thing with their own eyes have told us harrowing tales. They have told us of men and women and children dying by the roadside, their mouths green from the nettles and grass they had eaten in their overpowering hunger; of others dropping dead after partaking of a meal of porridge which proved too much for stomachs long without food; of women carrying their dead husbands on their backs to the graveyards; of others, too weak themselves to carry their dead, burying their beloved ones somewhere near home. Dead vagrants, and they were many, were buried simply by pulling the sod fence down over them to cover them where they had died. Not one woman but many, ill with fever, took the body of her husband who had died in the bed beside her of the same fever and buried it in the cabin floor. Then she, too, lay down to die. All over the parish the graves of the famine victims are scattered, sometimes single graves, now and again several together. How many lie buried in the strand at Mulranny we could not count. Who they were God alone knows. There they rest, the fever of life over, the ebbing and flowing tides ever murmuring their requiem.

The effects of the famine in our parish were catastrophic. The population in 1846 must have been well over 12,000 and the number of families 2,700. In 1855, Griffith published his Book of Valuations. In that book he notes every inhabited house and gives the names of the occupiers. His account would represent the state of things in 1850. Since 1846 the number of families had fallen from 2,700 to 890, and the total population from 12,000 to something around 4,000. How many died of famine and cholera we cannot estimate, possibly some thousands. But to famine and cholera was added the landlords' campaigns of eviction. Lord Sligo flung some 40 families on the roadside in Treenbeg and Treenlar and thereby created his Treenlar Farm. It was his intention to evict his Lettermoghera tenants to form a Lettermoghera Farm. Sir Richard O'Donnell was also active. He declared he would not leave a Catholic between Knocknabola bridge and the river of Newport. He carried out his threat as far as he could but he, too, was baulked. Sligo and O'Donnell are gone and the hated Catholics are back again on the lands of their forefathers.

The famine provided the Protestant Church Mission with what looked like a golden opportunity. They set up soup schools at Pollaphuca in Kilbride, a place still sometimes called *The Colony,* at Rosgalive, at Murrevagh, at Mulranny and on the Achill road to the west of Mulranny. At these schools there was soup galore for every poor starving creature who was prepared to deny his faith. No others could share. This vile traffic in souls was an utter failure. Not even one apostatised. The final defeat of the soupers was largely due to direct action on the part of Richard Staunton of Roskeen. One evening in 1853 Richard met the Rosgalive Scripture Reader at Bunamucka Lough and thoroughly threshed him. The Scripture Reader took the hint and promptly retired to the more congenial atmosphere of Dugort. In the *Achill Herald* of June 1855, and in his book, *The Island of Saints and Scholars, 1855,* you will find Nangle's version of this incident. In after years Richard always claimed that it was he, under God, who had saved the faith in Tíranáir.

The religious controversies of the period are vividly illustrated in a booklet of 162 pages published in 1852, entitled *David* and *Goliath or The Complete Victory of a Mayo Hedge-School Pupil over Sir Thomas Dross, a Souper Knight, and Three Bible and Tract-Distributing Ladies.* The work was issued from "Grace O'Malley's Castle, 12th July, 1852." The author is Hugh Joseph O'Donnell, "a Mayo Catholic Layman." He was a native of Tíranáir. The Flynns of Fauleens claim him as a relation. The booklet is in English but the author evidently knew his Irish well. He was also a Classical scholar and was quite at home in theology and ecclesiastical history. His book is written in the form of a dialogue, covering several days, between a seventeen year old pupil of the hedge-school in Grace O'Malley's Castle and four Soupers, a man and three women. The Bible and devotion to Our Blessed Lady are the chief subjects under discussion. We must remember that, in those days, the Bible Readers and the other paid myrmidons of the Irish Church Missions were making it a special point of their programme to attack the Blessed Virgin and hold her up to blasphemous ridicule. The Bible, as the sole rule of faith, came next on the list. No home was free from the intrusions of the Bible Reader. Willy nilly he would force his Bible down the people's throats. These are the things the hedge-school pupil deals with in his own incisive and humorous way. He ends up by making converts of his four opponents.

In the course of this debate we are told: "The senior boys in our hedge-school belong to the Parochial Christian Doctrine Confraternity, and this is one of the nights in the week when the children of the parish assemble in the Parish Church to receive religious instruction before the Rosary shall commence." It is probable that the catechism used at this period was Dr. MacHale's Irish-English Catechism, which was first published in 1843. Before 1843 and possibly for several years afterwards the book used was "Dr. Kirwan's *Irish Catechism,* published under the sanction of the Most Rev. Oliver O'Kelly, Archbishop of Tuam; Very Rev. Patrick Nolan, A.D., P.P., Balla; Rev. James Ronan, Professor of Logic, Tuam College. By Thomas Hughes." The copy of this little book which we have before us is the 6th edition, printed in 1845. It belonged to Patt Fergus, Ardagh. How long before Archbishop O'Kelly's death in 1834 the first edition appeared is not known. The language of this catechism is entirely Irish but printed in phonetic Roman type, e.g., *An Tagus Chriosduigh . . . Ananim an Ahir agus an Vic agus an Spioraid Naofa. Amen.* In this parish, as elsewhere, the people were unable to read or write the Irish which was their every day speech. That was not their fault. The Penal Laws had for 200 years deprived them of every chance of education. It was a felony to establish an Irish Catholic school; it was a felony to teach in such a school. When the Penal era at length passed and schools could be legally established there were no

Irish text books, and few teachers who could teach Irish reading or writing. The so-called *National* schools did nothing to help. It was rather their purpose to destroy the national language, and in this, as we know only too well, they were largely successful. In spite of all, however, some of our parishioners in some way or other, probably in the hedge-schools, learned to read and write Irish. We have evidence of that in a manuscript notebook of the Stations of the Cross which was in use in Newport Church in the middle of the last century. The author is unknown. The prayers and meditations on the Stations are written in an educated hand and, apart from a few odd spellings, are a model of perfectly grammatical and idiomatic Irish. This little note-book is very much thumbed.

FENIANISM

IN the State Paper Office in Dublin is a dossier of some 30 documents dealing with Fenianism in Newport from 1866 to 1869. The first document is a list of 25 persons suspected of being Fenians. Head Constable Thomas Clarke supplied the list to Dublin Castle, 20 February, 1866. The first name given is Daniel Kilroy, carpenter, reputed Centre for locality. Then come John Moran, shoemaker, returned from U.S.A., said to be Sub-Lt. in an American Fenian regiment; Charles Garvey, baker, returned American; Patrick Moran, leather merchant; William Chambers, Gortfahy, served in U.S.A. navy; John Chambers, who had been in the U.S.A.; John Murtagh, Bunahowna, ex-U.S.A. navy; James Burke, Kilbride, frequents England. The only ground of suspicion in each and every case is given by Clarke as "common repute."

Clarke reported again on the 28th February that in April, 1865, Patrick Moran got a copy of the *Chicago Times* which had a list of Mil. Fenian officers, among whom was named John Moran as Lieut. or Sub.Lt. Patrick Moran had then a brother in America. The brother has now returned to Newport. After the Suspension of the Habeas Corpus Act he was in hiding from the police, along with Daniel Kilroy, from Monday to Thursday. Clarke suggests that a certain five of the 25 suspects be arrested in the hope of frightening them into giving information.

On 29th March, Clarke reports that Sir Richard O'Donnell is active against all suspected Fenians, and has dismissed his gardener and his steward. The latter is also Relieving Officer. Sir Richard will try to dismiss him from that office. Sir Richard succeeded.

Two police took notes of a sermon preached by Rev. John Concannon, C.C., in Newport Church on Sunday, 15th April. In his sermon, the priest said that with Fenianism he had nothing to do; let the authorities put it down, if they would or could. He believed there was not one Fenian in the parish, in spite of the report that the place was full of them. He said that every machination had been employed to bring them like innocent lambs to the slaughter but without success. The failure annoyed the authorities. He said there was a certain person (no name given) who was suspected of giving the list of suspected Fenians to the police. It was wrong to charge a person when there was no proof of guilt, but he felt it right to caution the people against believing that man now when he comes forward and says he saved the people from being prosecuted and hanged. Let time prove the case as it ought and should. Here a man named - (the suspected person alluded to in Mr. Concannon's address) stepped across the rails in front of the altar, and the discourse terminated.

On 28th July, 1866, Clarke reported that Patrick Moran, shoemaker and leather merchant, had received a newspaper from America, etc.

Apparently, no evidence could be got against our Fenians but they were there without a doubt. Things livened up again on 23rd January, 1868. The military in Castlebar were requested by the Newport police to take charge of four small casks of powder, ½ cwt. of fine powder in canisters, and fuse and cartridges. Martin Carey wanted them in safe keeping. This was on 13th January. The military waited till 21st January to say they agreed. There must have been some leak in the R.I.C., because on the night of the 22nd the whole store of powder, etc., was stolen.

On the 24th January, Resident Magistrate Stritch had to leave his warm bed in Castlebar at 6 a.m. and hie for Newport. The poor police, under his command, worked as they never had before. The powder was traced to an empty house. Full stop here. But the searchers spread out and behold a clue in the shape of a flask of gunpowder and a few grains of blasting powder on the road to Shramore. The grains led towards Treenbeg school. In the school itself were found seven or eight grains. John Flynn, the schoolmaster, long a suspected Fenian, was at once arrested. Later the following were "taken into custody on suspicion": John Malley, eggler; John Rorke, labourer; John Sweeney, relieving officer (successor to man dismissed in 1866); William Forrestal, carpenter; John Moran, mason, and William Flynn, brother of schoolmaster; all six from Newport. Stritch asked for detention warrants for all except John Moran.

Stritch reported on 25th January that no more powder had been

Pádraig Ó Móráin

Uim

(56) 1 Das Mädchen ohne
(57) 2 Die Nelke
(585) 3 Gottes Speise
(586) 4 Die drei grünen Z
(58v) 5 Muttergottesgläschen
(58s) 6 Das alte Mütterche
67 7 Der Eisenofen
71 8 Der Trommler
(167) 9 Der Geist im Gla
(161) 10 Das Rätsel
(170) 11 Rätsel märchen
(177) 12 Das Meerhäsche
(170) 13 Der alte Grossvater un
(181) 14 Das Eigensinnige K
(182) 15 Der undankbare b
(184) 16 Die Schlickerlin
(185) 17 Die Brautschau
(186) 18 Das Lämmchen un

Bí locht le fagháil againn tamall ó
fhéin ar an méid airtriúcán ó'n
mbéarla atá á gcur amach le déanaí
'ó látair agus tá dáta cló, ve airtriúcán eile tar tú teact ó'n gcúm-
n. "An Cailín gan lámh" agus ríve-
scéalta eile Ghrimm. Ní veirtear linn
ciaca ó'n nGearmáinis nó ó airtriúcán
béarla a veineadh an leabhar so air-
ó'n mbéarla féin v'airtrigheadh é ba
canncrac an vuine a sheobradh locht ar
mar sheall air sin. Dar mbóis is veas
nár veineadh rógar litiriveacta eavair-
náisiúnta ve ríve-scéalta Ghrimm
vineadh mar a veineadh ve rceálta
hanr anveirron. Is fíor nach féirir
ríve scéalta vutcaraca na tíre reo
vo fágú agus go bruil riad le fagháil
go flúirseac i litiriveact na Gaeuilge
agus fós ar béal na noaoine irr an
nGaovealtact ac ní fágann ran nach
ceart riro foganta eile a tabairt vorna
páirtí.

Maivir leir an leabar ro tá an obair
véanta go cruinn ag Pádraig Ó Mouráin
v'airtrig ó agus is mó páirte ar ruo
na tíre atá buiveac ve vá bárr.

(Síve-Soéalta Ghrimm, an tOctmhadh
Leabhar, Oirig an tSolátair, Baile
Áta Cliat.) T.P. 28·8·'45.

⋯⋯⋯⋯⋯⋯⋯⋯⋯⋯⋯⋯⋯
...D A. DAY.

Nonni agus Munni, a fine story with a spiritual bias and of special Jesuit interest, has been beautifully translated from the German by Pádraig Ó Móghráin. The adventures of two young boys lost at sea in an open boat set the heart leaping with excitement. Designed, no doubt, for young people, this is a book that will suit anybody and everybody. A very minor fault is the use of the phrase " comh luath i nEirinn " on page 210. Surely an Icelander would never say this. L.O.B. *Irish Monthly, April 1941*

Reviews and work of translation by Pádraig Ó Móráin.

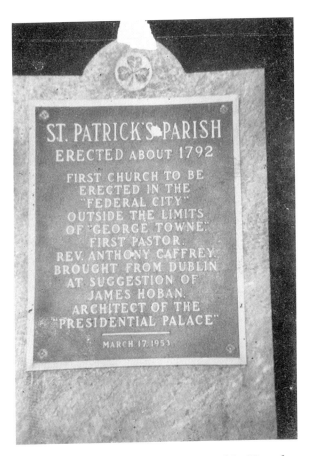

Memorial Stone outside St. Patrick's Church,
Washington, D.C., erected 17th March, 1953.

The fresco of Honoria Magaen
referred to in Chapter 7.

nonni aꞬus manni

Scéal breáġ uasal é seo a ḃfuil múnaḋ
doiṁin ann—cé naċ léir an múnaḋ de'n céaḋ
aṁarc.

Tráċtar, is sin go cliste ealaḋanta, ar
eaċtraí dá ndueaċa beirt stócaċ ó tuais-
ceart na híoslainne tríoċa; innistear dúinn
fá mar d'imṫiġ an ḃeirt aca (nonni aꞬus
manni) amaċ a' ḃádóireaċt ar an ḃfior ḋa
mór, fá mar ḃain taisme dóiḃ, fá mar tiom-
áin an Ɡaoiṫ iad amaċ ar ḋromċla na bóċna
fiorċmaire go raḃadar, fá ḋeireaḋ, i mbaoġ-
al a Ɡcaillte go deo. Annsin léiġtear, mar
móidiġeadar go leanfaidís lorg San Proin-
siais dá dtugaḋ Dia slán iad, mar ṫáinig
cat-long franncaċ de ċaḃair orṫa aꞬus mar
ċuaiḋ deáġ-sampla na Ɡcaitliceaċ i dtionn-
ċur orṫa (níorḃ Ċaitlicíġ iad féin go fóill);
mar tugaḋ slán saḃálta aḃaile iad ar ḃord
na cat-luinge Danṁargaiġe, an Fylla. AꞬus
'sé críoċ an scéil go ndueaċa nonni isteaċ i
ꞬColáiste le Cumann íosa 'sa ḃFrainnc.

A' léiġeaṁ an scéil seo ḋom ċuaiḋ mé ar
ais go dtí laeṫe geala na hóige nuair ḃí
"íosaꞬán is scéalta eile" 'á léiġeaṁ agam.
An uaisleaċt ċéaḋna, an ioḃairt ċéaḋna
aꞬus an t-ionnraiceas ċéaḋna atá mar ċloiċ
ḃuinn don tsár-scéal seo, aꞬus cé Ɡur ċeaḋ-
ċeapaḋ i dteangain iasaċta é feileann deáġ-
Ɬaeḋilge an Mióġránaiġ go h-áluinn dó.

Ar a son is go ḃfuil an clúḋaḋ aꞬus an
páipéar láidir teann aꞬus an prionnta mór
soiléiġte tá sé rud beag daor ar leaṫ-
ċoróinn, go h-áiriṫe nuair cuimniġtear
orṫa siúd Ɡur dóiḃ é. Meallfaḋ scéal den
ċineál seo buaċaillí óga ċun na Ɬaeḋilge dá
mbéaḋ ar a Ɡcumas é ċeannaċ—aċ níl
leaṫ-ċoróinneaċa ró-fairsing aꞬ clainn na
dtalamaiḋe.

tomás s. ó láiṁin.

---

mé féin aꞬus mo ṁadaḋ.

Is spéiseaṁail an t-úrsꞬéal é seo.* fear
ann aꞬus é aꞬ innseaċt sꞬéal a ṁadaḋ féin.
Ní madaḋ é Ɡur ḃfiú tada é mar ḃreaṫnóċ'
'luċt na madraí' féin air. Aċ ḃfiú go leór
é an madaḋ céaḋna sin do ḋuine a ṫuiꞬfeaḋ
an rún-diaṁaraċt a ḃaineas le ainṁiṫe—sé
sin do ḋuine a ḃfuil comḃuirde air taoḃ istiꞬ
do ċearcall na nádúire—i spioraḋ ar aon
ċuma. Is deas simplíḋe an cur síos atá
déanta aꞬ an sꞬríoḃnóir ar Ɡaċ áilneaċt a
ḃaineas leis an dúlraḋ amuiġ faoi an aer i
nꞬaċ séasúr don ḃliaḋain.

Is ciontuċ'ó teanga iasaċta an sꞬéal aꞬus
an loċt sin air a ḃíos go h-iondual ar a
leitiḋe—blas na bun-ċeanꞬaḋ. Leis an
Ɡceart a cur ar an Ɡceart níl an ḃlas sin ró-
láidir ins an Ɡcás seo. Iad seo a ḃfuil Ɡráḋ
aca do "ḃrionglóidí faoi'n dúlraḋ" is fiú
dóiḃ an sꞬéal seo a léiꞬeaṁ.

—m. ó. r

*mé féin aꞬus mo ṁadaḋ. Thomas Mann.
Tr. Pádraic ó móꞬráin, m.a. OiꞬ,
Díolta Foillseaċáin Rialtais. 2/-

Mé Féin agus Mo Ṁadaḋ. Thomas
Mann a scríoḃ sa Ghearmáinis.
Pádraig ó Moġráin a d'aistriġ go
Gaeḋilg. (Áth Cliath: Oifig Foill-
seaċáin an Rialtais.)

Is iomḋa leaḃar suaraċ, gan ṁaiṫ, a cuir-
ṫear ṡaṁ amaċ, aċ ní ceann den ċineál sin
an leaḃar seo. Scríoḃneoir a ḃfuil clú
mór air sa Ɬearmáin, aꞬus ar rud na
hEorpa féin, Thomas Mann, aꞬus tá long
láime an ṁaiꞬistir ar an scéal beag seo.
Madaḋ iongantaċ carranċaċ "Druaċair,"
aꞬus tá mé cinnte Ɡur maiṫ le aċan léiꞬ-
teoir a ṁacasaṁail de ṁadaḋ a ḃeiṫ aige
féin. Aċ ní h-é scéal "Druaċair" an
aon rud aṁáin aċ sa leaḃar, tá feall-

An tOllamh Liam O Briain.   4.2.'36

saṁnaċt aꞬus cainnt ar liaḋ ir ann coṁ
maiṫ, aꞬus cur-síos coṁ deas taitneaṁaċ ar
an iomlán naċ dtiocfaḋ leat an leaḃar a
ḋaol Ɡan é a léiꞬeaḋ go cúramaċ ó tús.

Cuttings of reviews from various papers.

Tales of the Wind King, by E. D. Laborde, is one of the best books for young people ever printed. The author, if I am not at fault, is a French Canadian. His story tells how the Wind-King came at night to young folk and carried them to distant lands, to see the sights and hear the tales from young people like themselves.

I have known this book for some twelve years, and have recommended it again and again, always being rewarded by thanks, and sometimes by toffee.

The last batch of books from the Gúm included a beautiful translation by Pádraig O Móghráin, that exquisite writer of Irish for children; but I should say *adaptation*, since the translator has made the travelling children Irish, and has brought out the Irish thoughts that every land suggests. I. Press 22-6-42

23·6·42.

Review in the Irish Press.

The shrine, erected by the people of Burrishoole, was, on the 8th June, 1953, in the presence of a great gathering, unveiled by his Excellency, Seán T. Ó Ceallaigh, President of Ireland, and dedicated by his Grace, Most Rev. Dr. Walsh, Archbishop of Tuam.

Newport, Co. Mayo.

recovered. He said that the houses of the suspects had been searched. In Moran's stable they found a horse which, apparently, resented the presence of the police and did his bit to show it; "One of Moran's horses is very wicked." Re Malley and Rorke, they are all and all with a suspected Fenian, Timothy Kilroy, who is brother of a "known Fenian," Thomas Kilroy. This Thomas, a carpenter, had got the key of the empty house on Wednesday morning, the 22nd, in order to repair it. He left the door thus: "the lower half of the door will yield under pressure without unlocking the upper half. Schoolmaster Flynn has been 20 years under the Board and is held in high repute by Mr. Brown, J.P., of Treenlaur. He has a big family. He has not been under suspicion up to this, though his brother, William, is a known Fenian. I held the schoolmaster to bail, himself in £50 with two sureties of £25. I recommend a reward of £40 for usual information."

On the 25th January, Stritch reported, in a second letter that after Treenbeg no trace of powder had been got and that all who had been arrested were discharged, "there being no evidence directly of indirectly connecting them with the outrage."

But the police were not to be deprived of a victim. On the 29th January Sub.-Inspector Hayes wrote that Patrick Moran's house was a rendezvous for suspected persons, that he, Moran, had with him for two years his brother, an ex-U.S.A. army man (now in America since last August), that he had been watched for two years but had evaded the vigilance of the police, that there was no doubt he was an influential member of the conspiracy, that the powder could not have been stolen without his knowledge, "and I am recommending his arrest." So, on 9th February "I lodged Moran in Castlebar Gaol … I found on him an advertisement of the trial of Timothy Brown."

The 9th March, 1868, finds Stritch reporting: "Grand Jury found three several bills against Wm. Forrestal. 1, for endeavouring to seduce the soldier Keane; 2, for sedition; 3, for common assault. When arraigned on the 2nd charge, Forrestal, acting on the advice of his counsel pleaded guilty, alleging in mitigation that he was drunk at the time he used the seditious language imputed to him. The Crown then entered a *nolle prosequi* in each of the other two cases and consented to his discharge on his entering into bail, himself in £50, with two sureties of £25 each, to come up for judgment when called upon and to be of good behaviour."

Meanwhile, Patrick Moran was prisoner in Castlebar Gaol. On the 11th March he sent a memorial to Lord Abercorn asking for release on bail, saying he had a wife and four young children, the eldest being five years, and denying he had anything to do with Fenianism. Another memorial on his behalf was sent in from Newport the same month. This was signed by Richard Prendergast, P.P.; Rev. John Concannon, C.C.; George Keegan, Prot. (recte Presby.) Minister, and a number of the parishioners. But the Attorney-General advised his detention on the 18th. On 2nd April, the warrant came for his removal to Mountjoy. On the 11th, came an order for his release on condition that he went to America. Moran replied on 15th that he could not go. Next day, 16th April, he sent a memorial to Lord Naas saying it would ruin him to sell out, that there was a case against him in the Queen's Bench, and that he had two apprentices who were threatening to leave him.

On 24th April, Hayes wrote to Stritch that he thought Moran might be discharged on bail. Two days after, Hayes and Stritch found the powder within 200 yards of Treenbeg school. But that same day Stritch reported to the Castle: "I do not think that Moran had anything whatever to do with the robbery of Carey's powder. In my report of 25th January, I gave it as my opinion that James Carmichael, Moran's apprentice, was the only person in the house to whom suspicion really attached. I am still of that opinion and consider the circumstances of the case tended to exonerate rather than inculpate the prisoner."

After three months in prison, Patrick Moran was released an 2nd May, 1868. But the R.I.C. kept an eye on him still. A memorandum dated 2nd May, 1869, gives a list of "persons who visited Castlebar without an ostensible reason that Sunday." The names on the list are: Patrick Moran, John O'Rourke, Patrick Cusack, Patrick McDonnell, George Quinn, all from Newport, and several others from other parts of Mayo, "those seven known to the police."

The raid on Carey's powder store has developed into a tale oft told but every time told differently. On the face of it, it appears to have been an official Fenian operation. As such, the man who had most to do with it must naturally have been Daniel Kilroy, the local Fenian Centre. Parish tradition has it that Daniel was the man. It took quite a number of men to do the work and we can be sure that Thomas Kilroy, who did such an ingenious job on the door, and Patrick Moran and young Carmichael, with many others, were certainly in the secret. Nothing, however, could be proved against any of them. No spy came forward to testify. Treenbeg school was selected as the best place to dump the explosives because the Kilroys were at that time engaged in repairing the building and they had prepared a hiding-place in the ceiling. The finding of a powder flask and some grains of powder on the Shramore road led the police to the school. All they got there was a few other grains. The local people all seem to have been in the know. The police were so threatening that Thady Horan determined to fling the kegs of powder into Loch Fiach. He succeeded in drowning one. Having done that much, he kept far away from the rest of the stuff. The police would never have recaptured the powder were it not that in order to save the people from further persecution it was at length left in a place where the R.I.C. must find it in spite of themselves.

Daniel Kilroy's name is not mentioned even once in connection with the raid. But being suspected "of being about to commit" some crime or other, a warrant was issued for his arrest. A friendly policeman gave him the tip. He got away on the train at Westport. He thought he was caught at Claremorris. The R.I.C. were there in strength to search the train. Into his compartment came a policeman who knew him well. He looked at the man of law and the man of law looked at him. No word was spoken. Then the R.I.C. man, going to the door, shouted to the others: "Kilroy not here." With a blessing in his heart for the man who had refused to betray him, Daniel went unmolested on his journey to the States and freedom. In the first list of men suspected of being Fenians, James O'Malley is mentioned. We remember him now as the painter of the three fine religious pictures which hang in the church.

JAMES HUNTER

ON Monday, 30th August, 1869, news reached Newport that James Hunter, gentleman farmer, of Newfield, Tír an Áir, had been shot dead near his home the previous night at about 10.30 p.m. The *Irish Times* of Wednesday, 1st September, reported that Mrs. Hunter had gone to church with one of the servants. On her way home her car had broken down. The servant took the horse and came to Newfield for help. Mr. Hunter took his gig and drove down to find his wife. He usually drove fast but, on his way home, at a sharp bend about 200 yards from his house, he had to go slowly. At this turn he was fired at and two balls entered his right breast. The servant, hearing the shot, ran to the spot and found his master weltering in his blood. Mr. Hunter died in an hour.

Except in one particular, this report represents the facts. The servant was in the gig with Hunter when the shot was fired. Having an inkling of what was to come, he tried to persuade his master to remain at home. But Hunter told him to stop talking, that he would drive himself. The *Irish Times* goes on to say that the only reason for the shooting was a dispute about turbary rights with some tenants. The matter had come to court and Hunter had won his case. He had also got a decree against one tenant at the Assizes, with £45 costs. "The goods of the defendant were seized the other day by the sheriff, and a notice which had to be served on the party, and which no one would serve for him Mr. Hunter served himself. Mr. Stritch, R.M., and other police have gone to the place . . . intense excitement . . . district hitherto quiet and orderly . . . two men arrested but later discharged . . . eight others arrested on suspicion."

"At the inquest held outside the dwelling of the deceased, evidence was given by Dr. Davis, by Mr. Hunter's son, and by the servant. Among the jurors were Francis Vaughan, foreman; John Curran, Roigh; Patrick Carey (brother of Martin Carey, Newport), and William Mahony. The verdict was: 'We find that the deceased, James Hunter, came to his death by being willfully murdered by some person or persons unknown on the 29th August.'" *(Mayo Constitution,* 7th Sept., 1869).

A reward was offered for information. Those who contributed to the reward fund included Sir George C. O'Donel, £50; William Pike, J.P., £25; Francis Vaughan, £25; Mr. Hunter (brother of the deceased), £50; Mr. Massy (brother-in-law), £50; Rev. Mr. Keegan, Presbyterian minister, £20; Francis Vaughan, father of Cardinal Vaughan, was then living at Rosturk.

Nine men were arrested. They were: Daniel Keane, Roskeen; John, Pat and Laurence McGovern, Knockranson (Knockmanus); Martin, John and James Moran, Roskeen; John Moran, junior, Roskeen, and John O'Neill, Newfield. Keane's name was Randal, not Daniel. He was a native of Glenhest but was at that time a teacher in Rosgalive school. Of the Morans, Martin, James and John junior were brothers. They were known as the "Fairlies." Their father was called Martin Fairlie. Fairlie is the Irish phéarlaí (pearl), a term applied to a beautiful woman - in this case, Martin's mother. The other John Moran was a blacksmith and no relation of the Fairlies. The three brothers had another brother, Pat. Pat was returning from the "hay" in England and met the prisoners and their escort at Burrishoole bridge. It was with the utmost difficulty the police were persuaded not to arrest him too, as a suspect.

The accused men were brought before the Court in Newport on the 7th September. On the bench was an imposing array of magistrates, the Marquis of Sligo, Lord Dufferin, Lord Wicklow, Lord Charles Bruce, Sir George C. O'Donel, Sir Robert L. Blosse, L. A. Norman, J.P. and Thomas A. McDonnell, J.P. Mr. Carr, S.I. for the Crown, submitted information and asked for a remand for eight days. Counsellor O'Malley opposed and said there was not a shadow of evidence to justify a remand. The remand was granted.

A fortnight passed. Then on the 21st Sept. the Court was again in session. The magistrates this time were: Sir George O'Donel (presiding), Lord Sligo, Lord John T. Browne, Mr. Stritch, R.M.; T. McDonnell, J.P.; Mr. Clive, J.P., Ballycroy, and Mr. Birch. Shortly after 12 o'clock the prisoners were brought in. Mr. Myles J. Jordan prosecuted for the Crown; Counsellor O'Malley (instructed by Mr. Alfred B. Kelly), defended. The first witness, Thady Keane, deposed that he did not see anyone on the road before or after the shooting, that he met Pat McFadden and his brother-in-law on the road at Mrs. Nobles (now McNea's at Castle Road, near which Hunter's car had broken down) about half an hour before the shooting; that the shooting took place about 10.30 p.m., that the moon was shining and that he heard a noise in the potato stalks on the north side of the road opposite the turn where Hunter was shot. Dr. Davis testified that he found two bullets in deceased's chest, one of local manufacture. Sarah Kearns, who had been a servant in Hunter's till the previous May, swore that James Moran had said to her that he would be coming soon to Hunter's wake. Thomas Connor gave evidence that John O'Neill had been served with a certain legal document. Another witness (who will be nameless here) gave the names of several persons who, she said, had used threatening language. "Some time ago I was in A. B.'s house. Jack O'Neill was there. Jack Grady was there, too, but went out. O'Neill swore that anyone coming 'keeping' on his lands that he would have his life." *(Mayo Constitution, 28th Sept.)*. Jack Grady and an old man, Micky Keane, were the first two men arrested by the police, who found them at O'Neill's house on their first raid there. They were released. The Court remanded John O'Neill, Martin Moran, Randal Keane, James Moran and John Moran, the blacksmith. The others were discharged.

On 5th October, 1869, the judges sat once more and the books were opened. On the bench were Sir George O'Donel (in the chair), Lord Sligo, Lord John Browne, A. R. Stritch, R.M.; T. McDonnell, J.P., and W. Pike, J.P. "Also present were: Rev. Mr. Prendergast, P.P. and Rev. Mr. Concannon, C.C." *(Mayo Constitution)*. Mr. Jordan, for the Crown, said he could produce no more evidence. So the Chairman discharged the prisoners. The crowded court cheered and applauded. But the Marquis of Sligo was annoyed. He said: "I see a gentleman clapping his hands. I should almost propose that he be put in custody. Such indecent conduct I have never before observed in a court of justice." The *Mayo Constitution* (12th Oct., 1869) writes: "The observation was supposed to have reference to Rev. Mr. Concannon, C.C." Sligo's chagrin we can understand. The power of the ascendancy was slipping. The day was gone when it was possible to make examples that would cow the people and preserve his class. The writing was on the wall and he knew it. Local opinion then and since has been that the discharge of the five evidently innocent men was entirely due to the fairmindedness of the Resident Magistrate, Mr. Stritch.

During that month of September, the *Irish Times* dealt very fully and objectively with the circumstances of the case. In its issue of the 16th it quotes an inhabitant of Slingen: "Mr. Hunter was not a bad man but he was a foolish one. He should have remembered that people cannot live through the winter without fuel." On the 20th, it writes: "The whole southern and eastern region of the peninsula (Murrisk) from the south-western shoulder of Mulrea, along the Killeries and the Errif river, up to Westport in the north-east, has been depopulated by Lord Sligo and let to Captain Houston for a grazing farm." In an article on the 12th we are told about James Hunter and his procedure in his Tír an Áir holding. Hunter, who had been stock-manager for Capt. Houston at Glenummera, took on lease from a Mr. Smith, about 1856, two glens in Tír an Áir covering two thousand acres at 6d. per acre. The other tenants had turbary rights in the glens, and the lease contained a clause, granting an abatement of £10 in the annual rent as compensation for damage caused by the tenants in cutting their turf. Some time later, Smith sold the property to a Rev. Mr. Gibbings. Gibbings either forgot, or was ignorant of, the turbary clause in the lease and Hunter did not get his £10 abatement. When this happened a second time Hunter, instead of approaching the landlord, took the easier course, as he thought, of forbidding the cutting of turf on his lands. As a result, the people were in desperate straits for want of fuel. In addition, most of the glen land was unfenced and trespass was inevitable. The *Irish Times* special reporter wrote: "I am told that the records of Newport Court are full of Mr. Hunter's proceedings against these poor people for trespass. Sometimes it was a goose, sometimes a donkey or a pig, more usually a calf or a sheep that

strayed on to Mr. Hunter's mountain. Sometimes it was the people themselves who took a short cut across his many-acred farm. The fines were as a
rule one or two shillings, the costs twice or three times the fine.

"John O'Neill's rent was £8 18 6. Hunter sued him for trespass and got
a decree for £8 damages with £40 costs. O'Neill was ruined. He had to sell
all his cattle. A distraint was put on his crops, and his pig was put to the
pound. On Sunday, O'Neill's wife begged Hunter, on her knees I am told,
for permission to dig potatoes for the family dinner. He refused." The report
adds that O'Neill had no gun and did not know how to fire a gun.

In her book, *Twenty Years In The Wild West,* Mrs. Houston, wife of
Captain Houston of Glenummera, says of James Hunter: "He was about 40
years of age, 6 feet 2 inches at least in height, broad-shouldered and strong
in proportion. His grandfather had the honour of being the original of Sir
Walter Scott's Dandie Dinmont." She registers her pity for the dead man's
orphaned children, but her chief object in writing about the matter is to tell
the world what she thinks of the barbarous people of Tír an Áir and their
hardly less barbarous priests. She was a bigot, indeed, but she was not
altogether blind. Elsewhere in her book she makes it clear that the *modus
operandi* of her own church and its clergy is not entirely to her liking. Her
words in this connection paint so vivid a picture of what the Catholics of the
west of Ireland had to put up with at that time that they deserve to be quoted
in extenso: "Our Boanerges (the Aasleigh Minister) is never deterred by any
amount of bad weather from the duty of attacking on Sunday afternoons the
errors and "idolatries" of the Church of Rome … On one occasion this stal-
wart defender of the Faith spoke of the Blessed Virgin as a 'sinful,
unrighteous woman,' of the Cross as 'a blasphemous emblem,' and of
Roman Catholics, both generally and individually, as hopelessly doomed
(they being liars and idolaters) to everlasting burning. Can we wonder that
when the gauntlet was thus violently thrown down - when strewed by the
roadside were frequently found printed papers containing the bitterest abuse
and ridicule of the priests; when Scripture readers, mission-sent, forced
themselves into the cabins and obliged the occupants, however averse to the

infliction, to listen to the Word of God - can we wonder that with such and many other provocations to wrath, the clergy should have accepted the challenge?" (Pp. 129-130).

Mrs. Hunter and her two children continued to live at Newfield for some years after the tragedy. The man who fired the fatal shot will ever remain unknown. It is, however, quite likely that all local rumours are wide of the mark. Nor are we sure that the deed was an act of local vengeance against a tyrant. It was possibly carried out under the orders of the Irish revolutionary executive of the period.

SLOINNTE: PAROCHIAL SURNAMES

IN Burrishoole old Mayo surnames predominate. Such are: Ó Máille (O'Malley), Ó Fearghusa, (O'Fergus), Mac an Mháistir (Masterson), Ó Móráin (O'Moran), these four being branches of the one stock; Ó Béara (O'Berry), Ó Floinn (O'Flynn), Ó Cadhain (O'Coyne), Mag Fhionnáin (Gannon), Ó Conmhacháin (O'Conway), Mac Cormaic (MacCormack), Ó Duithche (O'Duffy), 'ac Aodháin (O'Keane), Ó hÚbáin (O'Hoban), Ó Cuinn (O'Quinn), Ó Mearlaigh (O'Marley), Ó Muimhneacháin (O'Monaghan, O'Meenaghan), Ó hOistir (O'Hester), Ó Gréacháin (O'Grehan), Ó Garbháin (O'Garavan), Ó Conghaile (O'Connolly), Ó Maolfhábhail (O'Lavelle), Ó Lachtnáin (O'Loftus), Mac Giolla Ghéir (Kilker), Mac Aitigín (MacCattigan), Ó Faithche (O'Fahy), Ó hÓdhráin (O'Horan), Ó Cathasaigh (O'Casey), Mag Réill for Mac Neill (MacGreal), Ó Ceallacháin (O'Callaghan), Mac Firbisígh (Forbes), Mac an Chalbhaigh (MacCalvey), Ó Bradáin (O'Sammon), Ó Cuinneagáin (Cunningham), Ó Corcráin (O'Corcoran), Ó Muireadhaigh (O'Murray), Ó Moolruaidh (Mulgrew), Mac Niocail (Nixon).

The Danes were in control of Clew Bay and its mainland for a long period in the 9th and 10th centuries but left no names behind them, if we except that of their chief, Ketill, after whom their stronghold is called Inis Coitil. In the 13th and 14th centuries the Normans got possession of Burrishoole. As a result, Norman names are widespread. The ruling family, de Burgo, became very Irish and changed their name to de Búrca, de Búrc, sometimes 'a Búrc (Burke, Bourke). The son of John de Burgo adopted the surname Mac Sheóinín (Jennings); the son of Gibbon de Burgo became Mac Ghiobúin (Gibbons); whether Mac Philibín (Philbin) comes from Philpin de Burgo or Philpin Barrett is disputed; from Paddan Barrett comes the name Mac Pháidín (MacFadden, Fadden, Fadian, Padden). Mac Pháidín is also an Irish Donegal surname. Other Norman names are Bairéad (Barrett), Mac Éil (MacHale), de Cliontúin (Clinton), de Cíomhsóg, Cíosóg (Cusack), Réid

(Reid, Reed), Mac Gearailt (FitzGerald), Seoighe (Joyce), de Brún (Browne), de Róiste (Roach), Mac Éinrí (MacHenry, Henry), Stondún (Staunton); (the Stauntons who murdered the Earl of Ulster in Lough Mask changed their name to Mac an Mhílidh, MacEvilly); Breathnach (Walsh), Mac Shiúrtáin (Jordan), Ruiséal (Russell), Tóibín (Tobin), Míolóid (Mylotte), Mac Coistealbhaigh (Costello).

The names Mac Suibhne (MacSweeney, Sweeney) and Mac Dhomhnaill (MacDonnell) were introduced by soldiers from the Scottish Isles in the 15th century. In the following century some of the Ó Ceallaigh (O'Kelly) family of Hy Maine in east Galway settled in Tíranáir. With the O'Kellys came other Hy Maine families: Ó Maolchróin (O'Mulchrone), Ó Canáin (O'Cannon), Ó Conraoí (Ó Conroy), Ó Tréasaigh (O'Tracey).

The years 1654-1660 brought a big influx of new names to the parish. Under Cromwell's inhuman Transplantation Law hundreds of Catholic families were evicted from their homes in Donegal and west Ulster, and driven like cattle to Mayo. Many of those Ulstermen settled in Burrishoole, and their names are still with us. Such are Ó Domhnaill (O'Donnell), Ó Cléirigh (O'Cleary, Clarke), Ó Gallchobhair (O'Gallagher), Ó Baoighill (O'Boyle), Mac Daeid (MacDaid, Davitt), 'ac Eachmharcaigh (MacCafferkey, Cafferkey), Ó Duibhidhir (O'Dever), Ó Cearbhalláin (O'Carolan), Ó Doighre (O'Dyra), Mag Fhionnghaile (Ginnelly), Mac an Fhailghigh (MacNally), Maguidhir (Maguire), Mac Meanman (MacManamon), Mag Íontaigh (Maginty, Ginty), Ó Dochartaigh (O'Doherty), Mac an Ultaigh (MacNulty), Mac Lochlainn (MacLoughlin), Mac Néidhe (MacNea), Mac Niallghusa (MacNealis, Nealis), Ó Piotáin (O'Patten), Ó Cíaráin (O'Carey), Mac Conghaile (Mac Neela), Mag Fhloinn (MacGlynn),Ó Maolmhaodhóg (O'Mulloy), Ó Muirgheasáin (O'Morrisson, Brice), Ó Catháin (O'Keane), Ó Corragáin (O'Corrigan), Ó Donnghaile (O'Donnelly), Mag Aodha (Magee, MacGee), Ó Neill (O'Neill).

Some time in the 18th century other Ulster families moved to the west and took up residence in the parish. From Breifne came Ó Raghallaigh (O'Reilly), Ó Sirideáin (O'Sheridan), Mag Shamhradháin (MacGovern); Ó

Loinn (O'Lunn), from Antrim, Mac Aonghusa (MacGuinness) from Down; Mac Canna (MacCann), Ó hÍr (O'Haire), Mac Shitric (MacKetterick, MacKitrick), from Armagh; Ó Daimhín (O'Devine), Mac Ghiolla Ruaidh (Kilroy) and Seambars (Chambers) probably from Tyrone or Fermanagh. There are some who hold that the first Chambers to settle here was an officer in Cromwell's army.

The following fine old Connacht names may have been here for centuries: Mag Oireachtaigh (MacGeraghty, Geraghty), Ó Conchobhair (O'Connor), Ó Léanacháin (O'Leneghan), Ó Dálaigh (O'Daly), Ó hAllmhuráin (O'Halloran), Mac Giolla Chaoin (Kilcoyne), Ó Marcacháin (Ryder), Ó Nuadháin (O'Noone), Mac an tSaoir (MacIntyre), Ó Liatháin (O'Lyons), Ó hÉilidhe (O'Healy), Mac Diarmada (MacDermott), Mac Aodha (MacHugh, Hughes), Ó Lodáin (O'Ludden), Ó Laoidhigh (O'Lee), Mac Amhalghaidh (MacAuley, Cowley), Ó hAinle (O'Hanley), Ó Maonaigh (O' Meaney), Mac Dhonnchadha (MacDonagh), Ó Maoileóin (O'Malone).

We have several ancient Irish names of non-Connacht origin: Ó Coileáin (O'Collins), Cork; Ó Cochláin (O'Coughlin), Cork; Ó Maoldhomhnaigh (O'Moloney), Clare; Ó Riagáin (O'Regan), Meath; Ó Nualláin (O'Nolan), Carlow; Ó Breacáin (O'Bracken), Offaly; Ó Mórdha (O'Moore), Leix; Ó Maolchraoibhe (Rice, Ryce), Oriel, or Rís (Ryce), Anglo-Norman; Ó Corbáin (O'Corbett), Munster (in Mayo, the Irish form is Corbaid); Ó Muireagáin (O'Morgan), Westmeath.

Families most numerous at present: Moran, 34; Chambers, 29; O'Malley, 27; O'Donnell, 13; MacManamon, 14.

LOG-AINMNEACHA: PLACENAMES

ÁRDACH (Ardagh), rising ground; Abhainn Gharbh (Owengariv), rough river; Abhainn Bhuí (Owenwee), yellow river; Abhainn na Daraí Duibhe (Owennadaraduive), river of the black oak, Newport River; Bun na hAbhna (Bunahowna), mouth of the river; Bocmhagh (Buckagh), plain of the deer; Baile Ó bhFiacháin (Baileoveehaun), Newport today; Béal an Chreachaire (Bellacragher), pass of the plunderer;

Carraig an Chabhlaigh (Carrigahowley), rock of the fleet (fleet of Gráinne Ní Mháille); An Cheathramha Bheag (Carrowbeg), little quarter; Ceathramha Saileach (Carrowsalagh), quarter of the willow trees; Caladh Breac (Callowbrack), haven of the trout; Camchluain (Comploon), crooked meadow; Carraig an Éadaigh (Carrickaneady), rock of the cloth; Cnoc Mhághnuis (Knockmanus), Manus's hill; Cnoc Bréige (Knockbreaga), hill of falsehood; Cnoc an Tobair (Knockatubber), hill of the well, St. Dominick's Well (Tobar Doimnic); Cnoc an Ghuaire (Knockaguaire), Sandymount; Cnoc Garbh (Knockgariv), rough hill, on shoulder of Nephin Beag, 1356 feet high; Cnoc Luachra (Knockloughra), hill of the rushes; Cnoc an Ghainimh (Knockaganny), Sandhill; Cnoc an Iolra (Knockanilra), Mount Eagle; Cnoc na Teineadh Aoil (Knocknatinnyweel), hill of the limekiln; Cill Bhríghde (Kilbride), St. Brigid's church; Cill tSárnait (Kiltarnet), church of St. Sarnat; Cillín Bhréanainn (Killeen-Breanann), St. Brendan's church, cemetery; Cluain Íseal (Clooneeshil), low meadow; Coill Mhór (Cuilmore), big wood; Cois Leice (Cushlecka), beside the rock; Corrán Buí (Corraunboy), yellow hook (in Derrada); Coirrín (Coreen), little peak, in Shramore: in Coreen's deep caves many a bale of smuggled goods was hidden in days gone by;

Dumhach Bheag (Dooghbeg), little sandhill; Doire Chúl Droma (Derrycooldrom), oakwood behind the ridge; Doire Fhada (Derrada), long oakwood; Doire Gharbh (Derrygariv), rough oak wood; Doire Leathan (Derrylahan), wide oakwood; Doire an Choill (Derrykell), oakwood with the hazel tree; Grafaidh (Graffy), dried boglands; Doire Lóchain (Derrylohan), oakwood of dried grass, maybe Lohan's oakwood; Doire Chlaoiteach (Derrycleetagh), wasted oakwood; Doire an tSagairt (Derintagart), oakwood of the priest; Dún Trusc (Doontrusk), Trusk's fort; Dubhchoill (Doughill), black wood; Druim Dreas-choille (Drumdrastle), ridge of bramble thicket (?) Drumbrastle is the modern name. It includes Acres (Acraí) and was formerly church land called Fearann na hEaglaise. Acraí is the same thing, Acraí na hEaglaise.

Eas, waterfall: An tEas (An chass), The Salmon Leap; Fáilíní (Fauleens), little hedges; Fraoch-Oileán (Freaghillaun), heath island; Gleann dá Thorc (Glendahork), glen of the two wild-boars; Gleann na mBó (Glenamoo), glen of the cows, given wrongly as Glenamong in all maps since 1839; Gort Uí Fhaithche (Gortfahy), Fahy's field;

Inis an Chnuic (Inishacrick), isle of the hill; Inis Bó Boineann (Inishbobunnan), isle of the heifers; Inis Cua (Inishcua), Cua's isle; Inis na Croise (Inishnacross), isle of the cross; Inis Odhar (Inishower), dun-coloured isle; Inis Iolra (Inishilra), isle of the eagle; Inis Tiobraid (Inishtubrid), isle of the wells;

Leitir Chaoin (Letterkeen), pleasant hillside; Leitir Loch (Letterlough), hillside of lakes; Leitir Machaire (Lettermaghera), extensive hillside; Leith-cheathramha (Leharrow), half-quarter; Lios na Gaoithe (Lisnageeha), fort of the wind; Log an Aifrinn (Luganaffrin), hollow of the Mass. This place is near the top of Torklieve mountain in Shramore. Near it on the south-eastern slope of the same mountain is the Watching Stone, Cloch an Amhairc (Cloughanawirk), where the guard was set to warn priest and people of the approach of the English priest hunters. The fact that a priest could celebrate Mass only on the top of a high mountain, and even then find it necessary to place a guard, brings home to us the relentless persecution priests and people were subjected to in Cromwellian and later times. Loch na mBarún (Loughnamaroon), Lake of the Baronies, here the baronies of Erris, Tirawley and Burrishoole meet; Loch na mBreac Caoch (Loughnamrackkeagh), lake of the blind fish; Loch Sceathach an Drantáin (Loughsgahaghadrantaun), lake of the humming hawthorns; Leabaidh Dhiarmada 's Ghráinne, usually called Lyobby, bed of Diarmaid and